THE LIFE AND TIMES
of the
IMMIGRANT
NURSE
IN THE USA

THE LIFE AND TIMES

of the

IMMIGRANT NURSE IN THE USA

Pauline & *Blessings!* ☺

PAULINE ESOGA

Library of Congress Control Number:		2020906889
ISBN:	Hardcover	978-1-7960-9775-7
	Softcover	978-1-7960-9774-0
	eBook	978-1-7960-9773-3

Print information available on the last page.

Rev. date: 05/22/2020

To order additional copies of this book, contact:
Xlibris
1-888-795-4274
www.Xlibris.com
Orders@Xlibris.com
809559

DEDICATION

TO MY PARENTS GEORGE AND FELICIA.
REST IN PERFECT PEACE.

Acknowledgement

I will like to start by thanking the Almighty God, for this gift of writing, the power to believe in my passion and pursue my dreams in life. I could not have done anything meaningful in my life without the Faith, Hope and Trust that I have in you. To You Be the Glory.

A million thanks my awesome husband Festus, for his love, relentless support and compromises from the very beginning of our relationship till date. I have never taken any of them for granted. Thank you for believing in me and helping me to be the woman Iam today. Am eternally and sincerely grateful.

To my children, Chukwuma, Kelechi, Chioma and Obinna, you are the jewels of my life and I thank you for being there even when I have to separate from you during your formative years, yet your steadfastness, love and togetherness is evident today in the people you have become., You are my heroes and buddies, Mom loves you all so much.

To Debby, and Felices, who started this journey with me, but had to retreat due to circumstances beyond your control. Thank you for some of the insights, thoughts, ideas and willingness to tell the story. That was my determination to continue and finish. Thank you for your support.

To my brothers and sisters, thank you for sharing my life with you when we grew up together. Each of you made a lot of impact in my life that is part of who Iam today. I have indelible sweet memories of our family life and will never exchange them for any other. It makes me proud every day to have you as brothers and sister even the ones that are no longer with us. I cherish you and Thank you.

To Vincent, Augustine, Uzo, Josephine, Elaine. Dawo and Kate, you guys were the anchor for my smooth transition to USA. The story will never be complete without you. I hope my book and writings are something that I've done to make you all proud. Thank you for your love and support.

To my friend – Chika, Albert, Emeka and Rita, you were there for me at my time of loneliness, fear and anxiety. You provided everything that true friendship is all about. You will never be forgotten in my life and I love all of you and thank you for everything.

To Yvonne, Brenda, Angela and all members of Calvary Torch Missions Inc. USA, the fulfilment of another part of my life. This book could not have been possible without you. I cherish all the mission trips we did together, and the impact we made responding to the Great Commission. I love you all and will always have you in my prayers.

Finally, to all who in one way or the other share their stories, input and ideas in making this book a success, I say thank you and May God Bless you all.

PREFACE

This book is a collection of the real-life stories of one immigrant nurse who made her way to the USA, from Wushshi and the stories of some of her fellow immigrants who had similar yet different struggles in their lives as they made their way to this wonderful country of opportunities. The idea of writing this book was to tell a story that would otherwise never be heard. Although I had struggled to find time in my busy schedule and at times felt the project was going nowhere, I kept at it, persevering to make this a success as I understood what it meant for my story and the stories of other immigrant nurses to be heard. Every migrant nurse has a different story, different struggles, and a different background, but the bottom line is though diverse, we are all still the same, and you will very well see it in my narration and writing.

The book, in some places, feels like a documentary and in others a narration, but the more I got into it, the more excited I was to let it out. It has some intense, raw emotions that are all very real in the life of this immigrant nurse. As I look back at my life, I realize there is no room to complain or feel sad about the choices I have made or journeys undertaken—it's all good. Writing this book has been cathartic and therapeutic to me, and I believe it may do the same for the readers and even inspire them to tell their stories in the way they choose. I have not embellished anything and have not needed to do that.

Introduction

In February 2016, an article whose headline read "The U.S. is running out of nurses" stated that the country that has experienced nursing shortages for decades is on the verge of having another shortage. This impending shortage, according to the article, is attributed to an aging nursing workforce, the U.S. aging population, the rising incidence of chronic diseases, and the limited capacity of nursing schools (*The Atlantic Daily*, Boston, Massachusetts, 2016).

Reading this article headline brought back memories of the same news in the 1980s, when in my home country, Wushshi, the news that foreign countries (the USA, the UK, Canada, and Australia) were recruiting nurses to fill their nursing shortages spread like wildfire. Being young nurses, we jumped at it and started to seek more information on how to go overseas for work. Initially, it sounded like an adventure, a girls' outing on the streets of London or New York, with no strings attached. On the other hand, there were so many other reasons why most of us were ready to jump into the next available plane and head off overseas with our nursing skills and knowledge.

Nurse migration is as old as the profession itself, as witnessed even in developing countries, when nurses migrate from rural areas to the cities to work, leaving the rural hospitals short-staffed.

Nurses have moved from their home countries to neighboring countries to work for various reasons. International nursing migration became more prominent in the early 1980s because of the acute shortage of nurses in industrialized nations. These countries paraded immigration opportunities and economic incentives that were hard to resist. It is also worthy to mention that the dangling of enticing incentives and opportunities was aided with what some writers have described as the "pull and push factors for foreign nurse migration" (Kingma, M., 2007). Most of the "push factors," originating from the migrating countries, were mainly socioeconomic, political, and geographical, while the "pull' factors were mainly economic and educational opportunities, permanent residences in the recruiting countries for the nurses and their families, job stability, work benefits, retirement plans, and compensation packages (Chikanda, 2005).

The story you are about to read is told by an immigrant nurse who migrated to the USA based on the above factors and her life both in her country and in the USA.

Birth, Parents, and Family

In the early hours of the morning at a busy maternity health center, a young woman gave birth to her second child, a baby girl. As soon as she was born, there were songs of joy coming from the family waiting outside, the woman's husband, the nurses, and the midwives. The mother was still in pain because she had a huge cut given to her to facilitate the birth of the baby. She was a big baby, weighing nine pounds, and beautiful, and her first cry sounded like a song. She quickly started sucking her ten fingers, evidence of being hungry, and the midwife gave her a whopping sixty ounces of glucose water before her first warm-water bath. Everyone was shocked at how fast she could suck and drink.

The proud parents of this beautiful chubby baby were my parents, Okeke and Urediya, and their joy knew no bounds. Father was a truck driver working with a company that bought and sold produce crops within Wushishi and her neighboring countries. He was a petite man, about four feet and six inches, and must have weighed less than 150 pounds. He was a very loving man and hardworking, traveled to so many countries because of his occupation, and would do anything to ensure that his family was comfortable, had enough to eat, and, above all, obtained education. He would give up his favorite drink to save money to pay our school fees and was one of the earliest people in our village to build a house with cement walls, roofed with corrugated zinc, and ceiling boards to separate the roof from the main house. He bought a radio so that his family could listen to the news and decorated our living room with paintings brought from his various trips. He was an honest man and would never give up what he believed in, and his motto was that with good education, perseverance, and hard work, success will always follow. He always told his children that they could achieve anything in the world as long as they remained *focused* and hardworking. Father did not have any education, but because he traveled a lot, he understood the importance of good education, believed in it, and gave us the best as far as his resources could afford.

Mother was a housewife, a peasant subsistence farmer who tried her hand at some petty businesses, but they never grew bigger than to bring in some extra money for the family, enough to pay her bills in the village as well as provide some food items when Dad was away and our "feeding money" was depleted. She was a very beautiful, quiet, unassuming woman, the star dancer and singer for the local village dance troupe. She could sew (or should I say patch up) our torn clothes, an expert in taking some old ragged materials to make dresses or shorts for us. She made my first underpants from her old skirt and fixed a rubber band at the waist so that I could play with my friend, wearing something to protect my chastity.

She was a good cook who could make the most delicious meals with anything she laid her hands on. Occasionally, while we were coming back from school, she had already made some food that, most times, was not what we liked, but we really had no choice, so we ate to fill our stomachs. On one occasion, one of my brothers asked if we could have rice for dinner and that each time his stomach gurgled, he could hear it singing, "Cassava, cassava, and cassava" because that was all we ate. It is worthy to mention that cassava was the staple food of the village, and we could eat it all day, prepared in different ways.

Mother's response to him was "The stomach cannot differentiate between cassava and rice because once it is full and satisfied, it knows no better. It is with our eyes and mouths that we see the difference, and if one is longing for something they cannot afford, they will end up becoming a thief and end up in jail."

My brother was disappointed and promised that when he grew up, he would eat rice every day to make up for these times we could not afford it.

The baby's parents brought her back from the hospital, and everyone in the village had a gift for her more than the other babies born at the same time. People were coming to their house to see the beautiful baby who sang as she cried. They would sometimes wake her up and stroke her feet to get her to cry as they all reeled in laughter and joy. Ngozi's finger sucking settled for the first two of her left hand, and it was said that as long as she could suck her fingers, she would not cry. Whenever she was hungry or uncomfortable, she would let out this cry that attracted the women and children in the village because it sounded like a song. Mother said she was quick to give everyone a flash of her smile even before she was three months old, and those flashy smiles continue until today. Her parents were of the Catholic faith, so she was baptized and dedicated in the church at the age of five months. The Catholic parish priest's name was Fr. Paul McCartney, who gave her the name Eunice. Her parents were not really bothered or overtly impressed as everyone in the village called her by her local name, Ngozi ("blessing").

Mother always said that Ngozi was a very kind child, never ill except for the regular childhood illnesses, never cried when she got vaccination shots, and when all the children in the village had suffered an outbreak of measles, she was the only one who had not gotten the viral illness. She was already singing and dancing even before she could talk or walk, and her appreciation for music was evident in the attention she exhibited when the village women were singing or dancing in the square or in the church or even when songs played from her father's radio.

Ngozi's parents had more children—three brothers and three sisters, a family of eight children living in a three-bedroom house with grandparents who spoiled the children with gifts, protection, and care. One of the grandparents stood out among all of them (paternal and maternal) in the lives of the grandchildren: Inne, her father's mother. She was outstanding because she had so many qualities that Ngozi was said to have inherited—the bad, the good, and the ugly—and she loved her with a passion. Ngozi grew up having many nieces and nephews of her age, a very large family as Inne had seven sons. Whenever there was a family get-together, she would deviate from the tradition that when the chicken or beef cooked with the rice is shared, the eldest children take their share before the younger ones. You take your share according to where you fall in line with your birth age. Inne would make Ngozi take the first share before everyone and actually showed her the biggest share to pick. The elder brothers, nephews, cousins, and nieces would complain to their grandfather, who would chastise Inne for not following the cultural way of sharing, but she was defiant. She had no problems showing that Ngozi was special and her favorite grandchild. Ngozi did get a good bullying and sometimes beating for that privilege, and occasionally, the other nieces would refuse to allow her into their playgroup, which made her very unhappy.

Inne was a troublemaker and could start one at anytime. She was always making up stories to get other women and men in trouble. She would be the first person to go to the local police station to report that she was beaten up by a man in the village. The local police would come arrest the man, and put him in detention at the local courthouse. On one particular incident, she started trouble by blocking the road, knowing that Egbuziem (the local wine tapper) was coming back from his wine tapping. She never liked him, from what she had told the grandchildren, because he had insulted Grandfather at the local meeting. Inne had to get even. When Egbuziem came along, he removed the tree stump that she had used to block the road, and she quickly stood up to him, screaming, cursing, and yelling. Egbuziem just brushed her aside to get away from her, and instantly, she fell on the ground, rolling on the dusty brown soil, pouring dirt on herself, and she quickly ran to the local police station to make a report for assault and battery. Egbuziem was arrested by the local court officer and taken behind the counter. Finally, he slept in jail overnight, and his family had to find bail money, which was very hard for poor peasant farmers in the village. On another occasion, when Ngozi was about eight years old, Inne was unhappy with one of the village ladies, Abigail, who was an old maid in her late forties. The villagers would always talk about her in a derogatory manner because she never got married. They said that she had to be a witch. That was why she had never gotten married—because the witches she communed with promised to kill her and any man who married her. With that story in the village, Abigail never had any suitors asking for her hand in marriage. She lived in her parents' house, took care of them before they passed on, and had her own small-scale business of selling cooked and roasted peanuts. She was kind to the children in the village and would give them some peanuts whenever they visited her in her home. Inne forbade Ngozi and her siblings from going to

Abigail's house and one day made them return the peanuts she had given them earlier that day.

Abigail was not happy about this gesture, so she came to their home to ask Grandmother why she had chastised the grandkids for accepting kindness from her. Inne quickly told her that she was a witch and that she would not allow her to cast witchcraft on Ngozi or her siblings. Abigail muttered something under her breath, which was inaudible, but Inne claimed she had heard what was said, and as she turned to leave the compound, she hit her with a big stick that Grandfather was going to use in building the yam barn. Abigail fell to the ground, and Grandmother pounced on her, throwing punches like a heavyweight wrestler as she struggled to get off the ground. She pushed Inne off her, wriggled herself out, and got up to leave, and Grandma lashed out again. Abigail, in defense, held her hands and set her gently on the ground. Inne started to pant, fell on the ground, and feigned loss of consciousness. All the grandchildren started screaming and crying, thinking that she was dead, attracting almost all the villagers, who rushed in and started resuscitation by pouring cold water on her head and face. Abigail was perplexed, to say the least. She could not understand what was going on. Meanwhile, all the women in the family, including Mother, were sobbing and throwing themselves on the floor, thinking that Grandma was dead.

The village men descended on Abigail and, without asking, started beating her up with sticks and their fists, accusing her of using witchcraft to kill Inne. She was so beaten up that blood was gushing from her head and nose as they continued to hit her with whatever they could lay their hands on. As luck would have it, the village chief was passing by and heard the commotion. He saved the poor lady from the beating and mauling. Grandma had enough water thrown on her. She got up and staggered to the chair, with everyone happy that she was brought back to life. Abigail was rescued by her only brother, who followed her home, while all the attention was paid to Grandmother. The chief requested that Grandfather, Abigail's brother, and the villagers return to his house the next day so that he would settle the issues, and everyone returned to their homes.

During the night and early morning, Inne tutored Ngozi and her brother on how to tell the story of what had happened. She changed the whole story and made them lie against Abigail. She told them to say that Abigail had put some witchcraft charms on the peanuts she had given them. Inne discovered that they had the peanuts before Ngozi and her brother ate the peanuts, so she asked them to throw the peanuts away. After Abigail was expecting them to die from her witchcraft charms and did not hear cries from the family's home, she came to check and found the children with their grandma, healthy and happy. She then confronted her, asked why she had thrown the peanuts away, and started to chant her witchcraft incantations to hypnotize Grandma to scare the children into eating the peanuts. That was how Inne had fallen down and lost consciousness, and the children started to scream out for help. The story was rehearsed so many times that night and early in the morning. Ngozi's brother was not as fluent as her. Therefore, Inne told her to be the lead speaker. She was not going to speak under the pretense that the witchcraft charms were still on her. The village judges ruled in her favor. Abigail was made to pay penalties to the village men and women. Both she and her brother were ostracized from the village for ten years.

Ngozi was very unhappy and snuck over to see her before they had left the village. On their way out, she stopped at their house to apologize for pushing Grandma but stated her innocence. She advised Ngozi in low tones, when no one was looking or around, that she should never in her life lie for anyone because God would not forgive her.

"Lying is a sin against God and man, so always stand on the side of the truth like your parents. That grandma is a bad influence."

EARLY CHILDHOOD

Ngozi's early childhood was filled with joy and love from her family and the villagers. The whole family—her mom, grandparents, nieces, nephews, and cousins—would rise up early and be at the farm before six o'clock in the morning. The trip to the village farmlands was a two-mile walk, and they always left home early in the morning as soon as the cock crowed and would come back when the sun set. She hated the planting season because of the early rising, the walk to the farms, and the bugs and flies that were always biting her and caused a lot of scratching and itching.

Ngozi did love the meals in the farms because they were cooked right there, fresh fish or meat and vegetables from the river and farmland. One could eat as much as they wanted because there were not supposed to be leftovers. The pots, pans, plates, and cutlery would be washed in the river and hidden in one farmhouse for the next day's meal. All the children enjoyed the food, but when it came to removing weeds from the farm crops or planting vegetable and seeds, Ngozi and her brother would find reasons to cry or fight with each other just to cause a distraction from their dislike for farming.

Ngozi was very quick to make friends and harbored no ill feelings against anyone. When the school year resumed, the teachers loved her because she was very smart and submitted all her homework in a timely and complete manner (unlike her brother), participated in classroom discussions, and answered questions eagerly even if she was incorrect. Nothing was going to stop, limit, or hinder her from excelling. Occasionally, on weekends, she would go and fetch water from the village springs for her teachers, who were always appreciative and gave her some special treats.

Ngozi, though sweet, had some flaws in her character. She was very talkative and argumentative and had never lost a talking battle. She could, in little ways, start trouble and make up stories to become the victim instead of the troublesome one. None of the children in her grade could stand up to her when it came to talking and arguments. She was never in trouble, knew how to talk her way out of it, and, when others got punished, would go scot-free. The villagers and her schoolmates called her "Lawyer" and believed that she could never lose a case in any court, be it her parents, teachers, or peers and even the village courts. Her parents were not very comfortable with this behavior, especially when they got to know that she made up stories to get other children in trouble. They chastised her for that, but Ngozi was the local champion and not to be stopped.

On one occasion, one of her friends and schoolmates, Ugochi, stole another kid's pen from his schoolbag, not knowing that a second pupil had witnessed the act of removing the pen from the boy's schoolbag. The witness spoke up when the owner of the pen started looking for it in class and eventually reported the missing pen to the class teacher. The teacher took all of them to the head teacher's office to evaluate the report, and per the school's policy and procedure for things like this event, both the kids were sent home to bring their parents to school the next day for the final decision, which most times ended with expulsion from school. Ngozi got involved immediately and reported to the teacher that she did not think Ugochi had taken the pen for keeps but was just borrowing it for some time. She was Ugochi's friend and had never noticed her taking things that did not belong to her. This was not true because Ngozi had actually witnessed her friend taking the pen out of the boy's schoolbag and had confronted her prior to the boy looking for his pen. After school, on their way home, Ugochi pleaded with Ngozi to assist her in winning the case.

Suddenly, the victim and witness appeared from the other side of the road and retorted to Ngozi, "Your lawyer skills will not work in this case because I have a witness. You and your friend will be expelled from school for stealing that pen."

Ugochi was petrified, to say the least, and begged her to help her out. She stated, "If am expelled from school, my parents will not allow me to go to another school, and that will be the end of my academic pursuits."

This was also a challenge to the local champion who had never lost a fight like this one. Ngozi was prepared to show them her skills at lawyering. Ngozi took up the job to assist her friend but for a fee, which was that Ugochi would bring her dinner over to their house that night and for three more nights and wash her school uniforms every weekend for the rest of the school year. Ugochi agreed to the dinners but was hesitant about the laundry of the school uniforms because she did not have money to buy laundry detergent.

Ngozi would not bulge and told her, "Take it, or you are on your own," to which she reluctantly agreed. Ngozi made her swear by placing her hand on the Bible to abide by the agreement because she did not want any bad business, and the deal was sealed.

The next day, all the parents gathered at the head teacher's office. The class teacher presented the case to the head teacher and asked Ugochi if she had ever removed the pen from the other kid's schoolbag. She denied and pleaded not guilty. The victim immediately cried out that she was lying and that he had a witness. Ngozi, who was called in by the teacher at Ugochi's request, quickly interjected and stated that she was also a witness for Ugochi to corroborate that she did not steal any pen. The teacher was surprised because the previous day, Ngozi had emphatically stated that Ugochi removed the pen. How did the story change now? A lot of discussion went back and forth, and it was as if a decision was about to be made against Ugochi because the teacher was adamant about Ngozi's inconsistent statements, but one could not win a talking or argument race with her. She asked permission from the head teacher to ask the victim's witness some questions. The request was unfortunately granted and opened a way for her skills.

She quickly presented that the witness was an unreliable witness who had, on several occasions, lied about things in class. She presented to the head teacher that this witness had always been jealous of her friend because she would not allow him to copy answers from her examination paper during the last test taking, which caused him to fail, and now he was on a vengeance mission. She asked the witness to describe in detail what time, place, and manner Ugochi used to get into the schoolbag to steal the pen. He was not able to give a coherent answer because he was dumbfounded at the questions she was asking him. He neither was prepared nor had taken note of the time, style, or manner in which Ugochi committed the offence, but he had witnessed her go into the kid's schoolbag and remove the pen. Moreover, Ngozi was able to prove that when he had failed the last test, he was telling everyone in class how wicked Ugochi was for not letting him steal answers from her paper and that he would get back at her. He was actually threatening her, saying that when they would come to the stream, he would push her into the deepest part of the river to drown. That was the type of threats that the boys in school would make, if the girls refused to date them or assist them with schoolwork. Finally, Ngozi closed her submission by alleging that the witness was not even in the class during the recreation period, so there was no way he could have seen Ugochi take the pen since the incident was alleged to have happened during the recreation period. The head teacher, the teacher, and both parents were amazed and perplexed at the dexterity, eloquence, and confidence with which she had presented the case, and it was decided in Ugochi's favor. The victim was asked to go and look for his pen; he may have misplaced it. That was the end of the case.

Ngozi was very happy but also sad at the same time because her friend was indeed the culprit. She was not expelled from school. She paid the fee, and life continued, but there was one missing piece. The girls would have to go to confession on Saturday for Holy Communion on Sunday, and the priest would know the truth. The news spread throughout the whole village like wildfire, and Ngozi was nicknamed "Lawyer." Her parents were getting more uncomfortable with all these growing-up pranks, which was becoming like a normal lifestyle, but she rarely got into any trouble. They had several talks with her to stop her and had even threatened to send her away from the village to become a housemaid to a "wicked" teacher who lived in the neighboring city if she continued with this behavior.

At school, Ngozi was not only popular for her lawyerly instincts and skills but also the teacher's favorite because she was always ready at the assembly hall to recite a poem. Memorizing and reciting poems, scripture verses, and portions from a book was the hallmark of the Monday morning assembly gatherings in the school auditorium. Once you entered middle school age, you could be called upon anytime at the morning assembly by the head teacher or his assistant to take the podium and recite your poem or whatever you had prepared. This was a way to encourage the students to borrow books from the school library, use the weekend to study and memorize the verses or book portions, and not play away all weekend. Many of the children were scared to death if they were called upon to do the recitation—but not Ngozi. She could recite a lengthy poem without missing a line, and the whole school would be applauding. One of her favorite poems that she had recited in eighth grade was "The Six Blind Men and the Elephant" by John Godfrey Saxe. It was a long poem that she had recited with some demonstration, mimicking how the blind men touched different parts of the elephant. There was so much applause in the school hall. The teachers rewarded her with monetary gifts, and even the women selling snacks by the school came to the assembly hall to reward her with gifts.

In the evening, one of the teachers visited her family, and Dad was home from one of his trips. He told her father that he needed to take the family to the big city to get Ngozi a better education because her talents, intelligence, and future academic career would not be properly harnessed in a village school setting. Father agreed and started to make plans to move everyone to the city, where his job had its station and office. By the end of the school year—after their assessment, report, and transfer papers has been processed, Mother, Ngozi, and her siblings were on the way to Kasama, to settle and become city people. The whole village came out on that day, as they climbed into her dad's truck with their luggage and stuff. There was crying and wailing, especially from their grandparents. Her mother was emotional, but for Ngozi and her siblings, they were happy to move out of the village and into the city.

LIFE-CHANGING EVENTS

Once they had arrived at Kasama, Dad made arrangements to enroll them in school and got a little store for Mother where she sold foodstuffs, and they all lived in a two-bedroom apartment. All the children (five) slept on the floor in the living room or the other room, while their parents slept in the other bedroom. The beds were made of old raffia palm mattresses, with old blanket spreads on them. There were no pillows. It was comfortable, and everyone shared the space. One of the children would occasionally urinate on the makeshift bed at night, and that would get everyone moving away from the spot and cramping together on any dry side available, which was not much. In the morning, the child who wet the bed at night would take the mattress out in the sun to dry up.

The city school was a different setting. There were smart kids, bullies, rich kids, different subjects, and classwork. Ngozi and her siblings' struggled, but Dad continued to encourage them to remain focused. He hired a private tutor to assist them in transitioning better and more quickly. The first semester saw all the children fail tests in all the subjects, and that was very discouraging, but Ngozi was determined to show her new classmates, teachers, and school that she was no pushover. She indulged in more study times than play, went to the school library and borrowed books, and met the teachers during breaks to ask questions. Some of the teachers were unhappy with her sessions with them, branding her as "inquisitive" and "bothersome," but she was not deterred—no more failures in her tests. What would the children in the village school think about her, their star? Some of them would be laughing at her, while others would be wondering what happened to her. By the next semester, Ngozi passed all the subjects and was among the first six in her class, taking the 45th position out of the 240 people who were successful in the class of 350 pupils. Her brother had already gotten a position in the school soccer team, and boy, these kids were back on track.

When it was time to take the entrance examination for high school, Ngozi scored very high and passed, but her brother did not score well enough to get an admission. In this era, in her cultural setting, girls were not encouraged to get a high school education. The boys were the only ones encouraged and allowed for graduation to high school. The girls, mostly after middle school, would be married off to someone and start their housewife lives—learning a trade, learning how to sew, or just becoming housewives. Ngozi was so scared of this cultural norm and how it would affect her, but Dad assured them that any of his children who passed the high school entrance examination would go irrespective of their gender. Ngozi not only passed but also scored very high and so had the opportunity to go to an all-girls boarding high school. This educational setting was the bedrock that had shaped her life even to this day. It was in Ngozi's second year of high school that the Wushshi Civil War broke out, and that changed her life, goals, career, family, and living. No one could really understand what was going on at the city or even the village level, for it was only rumored that so many Southern Wushishi (a tribe in Wushshi) families living in the northern part of the country were "running back or returning forcefully" because they were being killed. The news had headlines about genocide happening in the northern part of the country. Ngozi did not come home with her dictionary to find out the meaning of the word *genocide*, and every attempt to understand it fully was unavailable. All that was rumored and heard from neighbors, children, and the community was how people had their heads cut off, and their families were made to carry the torsos of the bodies with them, that pregnant women had their bellies slashed and their unborn children removed and killed. People were returning in hundreds and thousands with deep hatchet cuts, having little or nothing left for themselves and their children. Stories were told about how families were missing or lost as they were made to leave schools, churches, and homes without getting their loved ones together. Ngozi and her brother decided to go to the city railway station, watching as many trains came in with loads of these returnees, called *refugees* (another big word that she could not understand). It was even announced in school that everyone should go and give assistance to the refugees/returnees. Surprisingly, Mother allowed them to as long as they came home before Dad got home from work. Mother also wanted to get some information to share with the other women in her group. At the train station, so many people were gathered, searching for their loved ones and returning from the north, though none of their relatives were among the returnees. Ngozi was filled with sadness and grief, witnessing all the sorrow and hopelessness looming in the air. There was not much to offer except to go to the nearest tap water faucet and get water for the folks who were thirsty. In a couple of months, Father came home one day to announce that the eastern region of Wushishi was now called Bende Republic and that the war had started. He appeared very happy and even told the family that he was ready to go and fight the bastard northerners for them to be free and have a nation of their own. They could not understand it because what exactly did it mean to be free? None of them knew nor understood the politics of a military coup. For the children, as far as they were living with their parents, could play outside with friends, and ate meals as much as was provided, they had freedom. Several weeks later, it was announced that all schools were closed indefinitely. The school buildings would be converted to military training schools and barracks in preparation for the Bende Republic soldiers to go to war with the Wushshi soldiers. It was taboo to mention the name Wushishi in Bende, and for a child, it was tough to comprehend how they had gotten to this point. The adults discussed the situation silently but with such fierceness and anger reflecting the seriousness of what was going on in the country.

As the war progressed, it was noted how bomber planes and air fighters dropped bombs in marketplaces, churches, and any place where people gathered. There was so much fear and uncertainty, and people were no longer moving around freely. Father suggested that the family return to the village for fear of the bombs killing them in the market, where Mother had a small shop and the children, being out of school, were going daily to assist her with her sales. It was agreed that Mother would make an effort in the following weeks to sell off her wares, and Dad would take everyone back to the village, but this never came to be, because two days after the decision, they were woken up in the middle of the night by gunshots and bomb blasts into the city. Everyone was on the run, and Father gathered all of the family into his truck, but by the time he had driven for half a mile, a huge bomb went off in the middle of the road, and they were all shaken and covered with the dust raised from the blast. Dad got them off the truck, and they had to walk home to their village. Children were missing their parents in the stampede going on. Men left their wives and mothers who could not walk fast. Dad put the youngest brother on his neck, and Mother put the younger sister on her back. Ngozi was made to carry a suitcase and her brother as well. They had to take corners and backstreets, avoiding the major roads, which the "enemies" were bombing consistently. The roads were crowded, but their father held them all together, and none were missed.

It was a three-day-and-night journey to get to their village. Their feet were sore and swollen, and they were hungry and thirsty but scared to death from the sounds of gunfire and bomb blasts. No one dared to complain because there were a lot of children crying, looking for their parents. People were dropping down on the roads from exhaustion, but fortunately, the family had moved very far from the warzone. Father knew all the hidden roads because he had friends in the surrounding villages near the city. When they had gotten to a certain village square, he asked them to stay in a deserted elementary school building with all other fleeing people while he went to find some help. Their feet were swollen, scarred, and bleeding. Mother made a campfire, boiled some water, and washed their feet. She applied some Vaseline cream and hot balm (Mentholatum) and asked everyone to put their feet on top of her body as she lay on the bare floor, nursing her own swollen feet. That was very soothing and comforting. That evening, Dad came back with three of his friends from the village. They brought the first cooked meals in three days for everyone to eat, after which they took the whole family to their houses using some bicycles as transportation. Ngozi and her family slept in the homes of Dad's friends for three days while arrangements were made to get them back to their village in the next few days. All of them were happy to return home, at least to see their family, especially the grandparents.

That experience was so frightening and scary, and Ngozi's

inquisitive mind had already started to hatch plans of joining the war in any capacity that she could serve. As the war progressed, the village became a safe haven for many refugees. The military would rescue fleeing people (men, children, women, and the elderly) from whichever city that was threatened or captured by the Wushshi soldiers and drop them off in the local church or camp that was opened and manned by a group of white Catholic priests and nuns. Every day Ngozi would go over to the camp to pray with the children or assist in taking care of the little ones as a babysitter. Her parents were not too happy with this activity because they were not sure whether the war would reach the village sooner. The reverend father (a white priest) decided to use one of the elementary school halls as a sick bay because there were many children and women suffering from malnutrition, kwashiorkor, and dehydration. The nurse (a white nun) and the doctor from the nearby hospital came daily to consult, and they were looking for people who could stay to attend to the sicker ones in the evening. Ngozi asked the reverend father if she could volunteer because of the huge admiration she had for the nurses, how they moved swiftly from bed to bed, touching the sick people, offering them comfort, hope, and medication. Ngozi got the job of supervising the meals and making sure that it was shared equally. She was hired to work as an assistant in the dispensary and wards.

The clinic, within three months, expanded, and more refugees were coming every day. Her parents insisted that she stop going there, but Ngozi pleaded with them because she really wanted to be a nurse. All the volunteers were paid weekly with "rations" or food items, because food was becoming very scarce. This meant that Ngozi now brought home every Friday some food items, which became a welcome relief for Mother, who encouraged her to go. Ngozi wanted to be like Rev. Sr. Maria, to be able to offer the same compassion, ethics, communication, and love for what she did. She wanted to be a nurse and did not waste any time letting Sr. Maria know how much she admired her. Sr. Maria took more interest and was training her to administer medications, do simple dressings, and assist the doctor on rounds. Here came Nurse Ngozi of Bende Republic.

The war lasted for three years, and finally, Bende surrendered to the Wushshi soldiers after so much hardship, killings, deaths, hunger, diseases, and refugee situations. Ngozi and her family did not return to the city again but remained in the village. Schools resumed in earnest, and everyone went back to the old school. Ngozi was disappointed as she preferred the city school, especially for the challenges it brought. She also wanted to go back and brag to the other children how she had trained and practiced nursing during the war in her village.

Life in the village changed dramatically following the civil war. Most of the houses were damaged from the numerous air raids that had bombed or sprayed bullets on the rooftops. People were advised not to drink rainwater from the rooftops because they were contaminated by the bomb and bullet debris deposited on them. They were all rumors because no one could support whether there was any scientific relationship to these instructions, but the rumors or news went around the village fast. Some of the local rivers and streams had either dried up or were no longer clean for human consumption. The local elementary school was the Bende Army Engineer Corps, where the famous Ogbunigwe rockets were manufactured, so the news was that the army engineers used the local stream to discard their toxic wastes that resulted from their manufacturing war weapons. The villagers were instructed not to use the streams or rivers for water. Water became a problem for the villagers, and children had to wake up every day at four o'clock in the morning to go to a stream that was almost five miles away to fetch water for drinking, cooking, and washing utensils. Ngozi's father dug a hole at the back of the house and collected floodwater when it rained. He would put in a large amount of alum (potassium aluminum sulfate) to purify the water, and it was used for washing clothes and bathing.

When the army engineers were closing down the barracks and yards after the army surrendered, there was so much looting from the storage area by the villagers. People were running and taking things in gallons, bottles, and containers. They did not even know what they contained. Ngozi's parents went there to get their own loot, and Mother brought home some gallons of antiseptic, chlorine, and benzyl benzoate and one container of some substance labeled "Poison."

The Caritas International Center, where Ngozi was volunteering, closed. The reverend father and reverend sister had to vacate the center quickly before the Wushishi army reached the village and possibly captured them as prisoners of war. There were so many orphans and sick children in the sick bay plus all the volunteer workers waiting for instructions. The priest and nun took as many of the children as they could who were able to get into the military truck that came to evacuate them. The ones that were left behind were given away to the villagers who wanted them. Ngozi really wanted to take one of the kids home, but her mother was hesitant since she did not know her parents or where she had come from. Besides, Mom already had six children, and Dad had no job presently. The priest gave all the workers keys to the storeroom to take as much food as they could and donate some for the people who adopted the children from the orphanage and sick bay. That was a huge incentive, and within hours, all the remaining children were adopted, and food items were given to the new adoptive parents. Most of the children were between the ages of two and ten. She could not imagine being adopted by people who took you in for food rations. It was not out of love or compassion. It was an opportunity to get a bag of rice, salt, beans, a gallon of cooking oil, and some cans of corned beef. Up until today, Ngozi still cannot bring herself to forget the events of that day, when it was announced to them that the priests and nuns were leaving and that the plan was to give away the children they could not take. They were able to take up to ten children with them, and most of those kids ended up in the country of Gabon (West Africa) and were kept in orphanages.

School resumed, and Father took the children to the high school for registration. The principal addressed all the parents and children who had come for registration. She said that the Wushishi education minister has advised high schools in the defeated Bende to admit students and upgrade them only one class above their grades prewar. As a result, the children lost two academic years and had to catch up. The principal said that all the applicants would take a preregistration test to ensure that each student was ready to go to the next grade (class). Next week, they should come back with pens, paper, rulers, and folders to take the test. That evening, parents were seen shopping at the market to buy writing paper and pens for their children. They would put money together and buy sixty-leaf notebooks and share the writing sheets, with each parent getting up to ten sheets of paper for their children. They bought a box of pens and shared it among one another, and Father brought home one pen and advised Ngozi and her brother to share the pen. The plan was that since Ngozi was the one reentering high school, it was her privilege to keep the pen and, when she was done with her test, go and find her brother, where he was taking the entry-level test, and give him the pen for his test. Ngozi's brother that night, during their study session, gave her a strict warning to make sure that she only used her own half of the pen and not write beyond that. He went as far as making a mark on the pen using Mother's kitchen knife to ensure that they knew where half of the pen ended. He retorted that he was aware that Ngozi would go take that test and start writing as if she were writing a book and that she'd better stick to half of the pen.

The tests came and went. Both passed and were admitted into form three (tenth grade) and form one (seventh grade). They went to school with no textbooks but one notebook that was subdivided into different sections for copying notes and one jotter that she had gotten from Rev. Fr. Paul during the war. The teachers had no textbooks. They taught from the old books they had in their possession during the war. There was not a known syllabus or class curriculum. By the end of that first semester, the federal government brought through the Ministry of Education books, notebooks, maps, and all the required textbooks, school supplies, and reading materials to equip and revamp the schools.

Ngozi finished high school and graduated with the ambition of becoming a nun. Her desire to be a nun had been developed while working alongside Sr. Maria during the war. Her compassion, dedication, and love for the orphans and children treated at the sick bay were very influential. She was so kind, pious, and prayerful that everyone around her was always convinced that she was going to heaven whenever she died. Sometimes they would be wondering what she would be saying to the priest when she knelt at the confessional on Saturdays for Catholic confession. On one occasion, Ngozi was tempted to ask her but had to be careful because she was also her mentor and boss. Mother was all for her becoming a nun, but Father did not want to hear about it. He would be giving his daughter away in marriage so that the other siblings would have more opportunities for getting a good education either from the dowry (money) or from the future husband taking up the responsibility of paying for their education.

After high school, Ngozi went to visit and stay with her aunt who was a teacher in the city, and of course, that was the end of all her aspirations of becoming a nun. The city life was catching up with her, a teenager/young adult in a big city, hanging out with boys and girls who were all out of school. Ngozi's aunt loved her so much and would do anything for her niece. She enrolled her in a preparatory class for the entry test into the university, and by this time, the influence of the friends she had made plus her aunt's love for lawyers made her change her mind and pursue a law school education and law as a career. Auntie Lovett paid for the test preparatory classes, which were not cheap, and at the close of those classes, Ngozi would head to the government public library to study for the test every day. At the library, she made a lot of friends, and because of her innate ability to talk, argue, and hold intelligent discussions, she was never lost in the crowd. In fact, you could say that Ngozi became the center of the party. Everyone wanted to be her friend, and before long, she was the toast of the street where Auntie Lovett lived. This popularity made some of the girls in the neighborhood jealous, and they began to plot some evil things to get her in some form of trouble, but they all failed because as it was well-known and proven, Ngozi was a good trouble planner and so was able to quickly catch them right in their tracks. Auntie Lovett was a good person who had her niece's future career and life at heart. She encouraged her to take some more tests to pursue and expand her career search, thinking along such careers as teaching, nursing, or secretarial administration while waiting for her dream career of becoming a lawyer.

A couple of months passed by, and the results of various tests started to flow in, and behold—she was offered admission to study law in the university. As a result, neither Auntie Lovett nor Ngozi paid any more attention to the other mail that came in with results for other tests. Her aunt celebrated the success and bragged to anyone who could care about her little lawyer niece. As time drew near for the registration, Auntie Lovett sent Ngozi to the university campus to collect the admission letter and the prospectus that detailed the course costs and requirements. She came back, and everyone was shocked at the amount of financial implications to get a law degree, so she had to return to the village and notify her father. Proudly, she returned to the village, and that evening, after cooking a good meal for her dad and mom, she announced her results. There were no congratulations or excitement from her parents or siblings.

Mom was more concerned about her aspirations of becoming a nun, and Dad just nonchalantly blurted out, "Where will we find money to give you a university education? Even if I sell all that we have, we cannot afford that. Besides, I have no property except this piece of family land, which will be left for my sons to build a home for themselves later in life."

All of Ngozi's dreams came crashing immediately, and tears rolled down her cheeks like a water fountain. She had somehow had the thought or mindset that Father had money hidden somewhere and hoped he would use it to pay for her university education, but the reality was that she had never known how poor her parents were. As she sobbed away, everyone got up and left the living room to go to their sleeping areas except Dad. She could see him crying but hiding his tears. He could not say a word. Surely, he appeared disappointed in himself, but he sat there with her until she could no longer cry. When Ngozi got up to go to the sleeping area, she saw Mother kneeling in front of the St. Teresa shrine at the family praying table, asking God for a miracle. She must have been asking God to provide the family with the finances to see her daughter through the university. Alternatively, she might have been praying for St. Teresa to make Ngozi return to becoming a nun, in which case the church would take care of further education. Whichever prayer that manifested first was acceptable for Ngozi at this time. In the morning, everyone had left the house before she woke up, some to the farm, others to the stream, and the younger siblings to school. That evening, her mother asked her to cook dinner and assist a younger sister with her homework. She was not a very happy camper but dared not disobey her parents because there was still hope that they could come up with a miraculous means of paying for a university education.

After one week, Ngozi realized that there was not going to be a miracle, and actually, there were no more discussions about the admission to university. Life continued as usual. At this moment, her plan was to return to the city. She could find a job and save money to go to the university next year. She sold the idea to her parents, and they were okay with it but not convinced, but Father loved Auntie Lovett and believed that she would make the best decision for his daughter. When Ngozi returned to the city, her aunt had other mail waiting for her and was unhappy that she had stayed away for two weeks. She had been offered admission to a teacher training college at Aba and a school of nursing in one of the schools in the region. Ngozi's joy was enormous. At last, there was some hope. Auntie Lovett advised that she accept the nursing school offer because it was more financially rewarding, and Ngozi could, after her training, start a business managing her own maternity clinic and birthing center. She advised against becoming a teacher because it was not financially lucrative. She may end up living from paycheck to paycheck like her and may never be able to assist financially, supporting her siblings' education. She said that teachers were poorly paid because their "reward is in heaven." She said that as a nurse, there was a chance of pursuing her dreams of becoming a nun, especially if, by chance, she would not get a husband in the future because of the myth in their town that nurses did not make good wives. She could still support herself and her parents and siblings.

Ngozi proceeded to the nursing school. After all the necessary interview processes, she was offered admission to a three-year nursing program. Auntie Lovett and her family celebrated this admission, and everyone was happy for her because of her dreams coming true of a nursing career and the possibility of becoming a nun. She finished her nursing education and passed the licensing examination in record time, but in the meantime, her graduation from nursing school was received with mixed feelings in the village. There had existed an unfounded rumor that nurses had the knowledge, skills, and ability to commit abortions. Therefore, young men were hesitant to ask for their hands in marriage. It was already concluded that they would not be able to have children. On the other hand, as a nurse, Ngozi knew and understood the impact it would make for the health care of her people. She would have the opportunity to work with the doctors in the local hospital and make her villagers proud that one of their own daughters could make health care available to them.

After graduating from nursing school, Ngozi secured a job in the general hospital at the city, the first disappointment in the village because of her moving from the village to the big city, but she was nonetheless happy because it would open doors for her to live in the city, get married, and advance her nursing career. She promised her parents and family to visit monthly to check on their health and possibly organize and educate them on some health issues and health promotion. She would educate them on healthy living and the children's health issues. At the general hospital, Ngozi excelled as a wonderful, caring, and compassionate nurse and received star awards in patient care within her first year of working in the facility. She was the star of all employees, colleagues, and peers because of her beauty, diligence, and compassion in the care of her patients and her relationships with her colleagues. She was always neatly dressed—and professionally too—that one of her patients gave her a pet name: "Stainless."

Within five years, Ngozi found herself moving along fast through the ranks and was promoted to nurse manager of her unit. She went back to school and graduated with a registered midwife license, as required by the Wushishi Nursing and Midwifery Council. Marriage came knocking on the door, and she was quickly swept off her feet by a handsome, sweet young man (Chima) from the neighboring village, and quickly, they were married—another change in her life. She married her sweetheart and immediately started a family. She kept her promise and would go to her village monthly and treat her people, checking their blood pressure and advising them to go to the hospital, sometimes driving them to her hospital for further care. Ngozi would accommodate her village folks in her home in the city to receive treatment in the general hospital where she worked.

Within ten years of her career, she was a nurse manager, a registered nurse and midwife (RNRM), and a mother of two children. Ngozi and her husband and children were living an average middle-class life and had built a moderate family home in the city and village, with the kids in private Catholic schools. She had a mini grocery shop business in the neighborhood. They were able to assist their immediate and extended family financially. She continued to advance her nursing career, getting certified in operating room nursing.

The Change

The Wushishi government underwent a series of military coups and instability that impacted the economy, causing the nonpayment of salaries for government employees when due. The private sector downgraded their budget, and most people were laid off. Ngozi's husband was one of them. There were no unemployment benefits whatsoever. Ngozi and her family became distraught. The mini grocery shop business was also affected because they could no longer refill their stock, so they decided to close the business and use the remaining items to manage their family. Some basic food was out of the reach of regular people. Most families, especially those in the health-care industry, saw open doors for migration to Europe, the USA, and the Middle East. Rumors and information relating to migration were circulating in and around the hospitals. Agents started to spring up here and there. Ngozi and her husband talked about it briefly as their economic life worsened. They finally pulled their children from their private schools. The thought of being separated from her husband and children, not to mention her aging parents, was not only mindboggling to her but also frightening. The reality was that migration could be the only chain of survival for all, and one thing had to be given up—family or survival and support for everyone.

THE DECISION

Ngozi and her husband talked to few people whose spouses had already migrated, and it sounded like something they could embark on. Chima had friends in the UK and the USA and reached out to them to assist his wife in migrating for a few years because there was a belief that Wushishi political and economic situation would soon be over. Some of Ngozi's colleagues had already migrated. She reached out to them for assistance, and they advised her to take some of the qualifying examinations and tests before proceeding to make it easier for employment opportunities. The family sold Ngozi's car for her to pursue the qualifying exams: the CGFNS (Committee for Graduates of Foreign Nursing schools), the TOEFL (Test of English as a Foreign Language), and the TSE (Test of Spoken English). Some of the tests needed traveling to the neighboring country as there were no examination centers in Wushishi. She traveled to the neighboring country, took the tests, and was successful.

Having passed all the qualifying tests, she reached out to her colleagues and friends for assistance with employment opportunities. Most of them did not respond, while those who had responded were not forthcoming with adequate information. In the meantime, it was getting more difficult having the daily basic needs met for the family. Ngozi no longer owned a car, the children were in public schools, and there was no steadier source of income for the family. Ngozi's present job at the general hospital had not paid any salaries for six months, and there was little or no hope for any payment forthcoming. Chima's friends were not helpful either in assisting them with getting a job in the UK or the USA. It appeared that all hope was lost, so "What next?" was the question. Chima had the understanding that migration may be the only way forward, but he needed his wife to be there not only for him and the children but also for the extended family. It was a hard decision for him to make, but as the head of the house, he had to make a decision about which Ngozi would agree with him because of the family.

Moving to America

One fateful morning Ngozi got a letter from one of her classmates who had migrated to the USA some years ago, inviting her to come to her wedding. She told her that when she arrived, she would get a health-care agency to file immigration papers to assist her in getting a job, obtaining immigrant status, and bringing her family later. She told her that it was the easiest way to migrate to the USA, and she would assist her with settling down in the USA, and in two years, her family would be able to migrate as well. Ngozi could not believe her eyes. This was a prayer answered and an opportunity that could not be missed. As soon as her husband came home from visiting their parents, she broke the news to him, and both of them set out immediately to get all the required documents as stated for the American Embassy visa application. Everything went well, and within three months, all arrangements were made for her to travel. The joy of obtaining visa passage to the USA and the prospect of the whole family living in God's own country, enjoying the life of "milk and honey," was the dream of the whole family. No matter how bad it was to leave their home country, it surely would be better than her country, where she had not been paid any salary for the past six months and was still expected to come to work daily.

As the date for her trip drew near, Chima was no longer excited.

He felt alone and was not sure how life would be after his wife traveled. He had some fear of the children not being taken care of, his wife abandoning him and getting into an amorous relationship in the USA, or nobody being there to take care of her. Ngozi's parents and family had mixed feelings of sadness and joy, especially her mother, who was not in the best of health. One of her daughters had been managing her health condition, and she was not sure who would be doing that for her. On the day of travel, a prayer session was held in the house. Chima, the children, and Ngozi were all crying as she left the house to go to the airport. Her last child, in fact, started running a fever. She had to stop and give him some medication and educated her husband on how to manage the fever. Ngozi arrived at the JFK Airport the next day, all alone, but her classmate Clara was at the airport with two other men who turned out to be the health-care agents who would file the papers for her to get a job and obtain a resident card called a "green card."

Ngozi slept so quickly, being tired from the sixteen-hour flight, and woke up from a bad dream. In the dream, she saw her husband and children begging her not to leave them because she was their mom and wife. She saw Chima on the floor of their living room, very sick, and she was waving goodbye to him and the kids, all watching her depart. She started to cry and wanted to call home immediately to let her family know how much she loved them and would never leave them, but Clara had gone to work. She wished that she had never left her country because her family was the only thing she had. What if her husband became sick and died? What would happen to her children? It would have been better to stay there and endure the hardships instead of migrating to the USA. What in the world had made her agree to come over here, and where was Clara?

She saw the note left on the table for her from Clara telling her to rest and eat the food in the refrigerator. She was advised not to open the door for anyone. Clara would be back at around 9:00 p.m., and she was working a twelve-hour shift at the hospital in Brooklyn. Ngozi became very lonely, sad, and dejected. She prayed to God for strength and direction in this lonely place. She did not know how to use the telephone and could not even call Clara or her family. She sat down in the living room, fell asleep, and did not know what time it was. She was even scared to look out the window for fear of someone shooting her from the window, as she had seen in the movies. She did not know when Clara came back from work, but this was her routine for the next two days.

Clara was off for two days but had to work at her second job. Ngozi marveled at how tired she looked and why she had to work two jobs without any days off. Since her arrival, they had never had a conversation about how she would get the job and the immigration papers and move ahead to making the dollars that she had come for. Everything was different from the conversation they had before she had left her country. On Sunday, she really wanted to go to church, but Clara told her she had never been to church since she moved to New York from Chicago because she had worked every day and prayed at home. After they prayed together, the two men who had met her earlier at the airport called, and they left to meet them at a restaurant, the first time she left the house since she had arrived a week ago. Everything appeared to her like a mirage—a *big dream*.

Ngozi and Clara arrived at the restaurant to meet the men from the hiring agency. They all sat together to discuss her fate. The men were from a New York agency that hired nurses with CGFNS certificates for nursing homes and hospitals with the agreement that the nurse hired would pass her nursing licensure board exams in six months before her visiting visa expired. The agency would file a

H-1B visa for the nurse, and if everything worked out well, the nurse should be able to get her green card(Residency Permit) in a year, and her family would be able to join her in the USA in less than two years. The fee for this filing sponsorship was $2,000, paid up front. At the same time, the nurse would sign a contract to work with the agency a year before looking for a job of her own. The understanding here was that as you worked for the agency, they paid you, and in turn would be paid , almost 100 percent more from the hospital or nursing homes they had contracted for you to work in. Ngozi was looking at another bad dream. How could she pay $2,000 up front when all she had come into the country with was $100, which Chima had struggled to collect from a friend who had returned from Saudi Arabia to visit his wife, who was a nurse working in Saudi Arabia?

She looked at Clara with fear and uncertainty in her eyes, begging for direction. At this moment, it appeared that her life and survival were in Clara's hands, but she was met with a cold "don't care" attitude from her friend and classmate. Clara told her that the money could be raised from a loan, to which she would be working to pay back in six months with a $200 interest. Her collateral would be her passport, which contained her visa and her return ticket, which she was supposed to send back home so that her family would get a refund of the unused one-way trip from the travel agency. She was scared and felt that something evil was lurking around. Clara had changed from someone she had known before, and no one else but her friend in Washington DC knew that she was in the country. Her friend in DC had gotten Clara's home phone and called her from time to time, encouraging her. She could not wait to tell her the next day, but she agreed with all the plans as her gut feeling was that this was her only chance to make it here. She was determined to survive, make it, and get her family to the USA. Her husband called twice a week. She talked to the children and told Chima everything except the money she had borrowed. Clara took her to Manhattan the next day to fill out and sign all the papers and contract, and they got the loan in her name as she surrendered her passport to Clara to give to the loaner. Once she had surrendered her passport, she immediately felt like her life had been surrendered to folks she did not know. She was scared. What would become of her dreams and that of her family? She was beginning to doubt her journey. Was this a mistake or a miscalculated idea? Ngozi started to cry, and Clara reassured her that this was the only way to survive in America.

Ngozi reached out to some of her friends in the USA as news of her arrival had circulated to her classmates and friends. She asked for support with books, ideas, and suggestions on how to make it here. She would leave the apartment in the morning as soon as Clara left for work and take the bus or train to explore the city and find something to do to keep her head together. She quickly found the public library and went there every day to read nursing books and prepare for her licensing exams. Any attempt to borrow books from the library was impossible because she had no identification card, and her passport was still with the agency. When she asked Clara how to get her passport back, she was directed to the Manhattan office to pick it up because they did not need it anymore and would not put it in the mail. How could she go to Manhattan? She had no idea how to get there, but as the weeks went by, she realized she had to start making her own decisions. Clara was beginning to feel that she was a burden and needed to move on with her life.

One fateful morning she boarded the train and followed the instructions written down for her by her friend. She arrived at Manhattan and walked for ninety minutes to find the office on Broadway Street. She was walking in circles and got lost so many times, but at last, she asked someone who assisted her in locating the address, realizing that she had gone past that building more than four times during her circling of Broadway Street. She was hungry, thirsty, and tired, but the voice of her friend telling her this was how to survive and the fear of disappointing her family kept her pushing on. At last, she found the office and met with the receptionist. She picked up her passport and, at the same time, met three other women, (Indira, Felicity, and Saba), all immigrant nurses on various stages of getting their immigrant status normalized. This was the beginning of phase two of her journey.

Ngozi got home and discussed her Manhattan trip with Clara and the ladies she had met at the agency office. She told her that one of the ladies promised to get her connected to a Jewish family to work as a nanny for two children, and she was willing to take it. Clara was not very supportive but rather advised her to just concentrate and pass her board exam. Then the agency would get her a job as a nursing assistant, en route to getting an RN job when her papers (work permit) came through. Ngozi was thinking of taking the advice, but she remembered that each time her husband called, there was a need at home to feed the children, pay school fees, and run the house. She needed to get any job to be able to support them.

She called Indira and requested her assistance in getting the job of a live-in nanny. Indira got back to her and took her to the home of the couple seeking to hire a nanny for an interview, in which she was successful. They offered her the job at a rate of $250 per week. She would live with them, and the only challenge was that she would only eat kosher food. She would work every day and get one weekend off in the month. Her duties included taking care of the children (aged five and three), cleaning the house, mowing the lawn, feeding and walking the dogs, and doing the laundry plus folding and ironing all the clothes. She would live in the basement but could sleep in the living room because the basement did not have good heating or air conditioning. The children were not allowed in the basement, so she had to stay with them in the living room and take them upstairs to their rooms to sleep, but she was not allowed to enter the rooms. She could read her Bible per her Christian faith, but the children were not to be told about Jesus. Ngozi had a phobia of dogs because she had been bitten as a child by a stray dog in her village and had to take twenty-four anti rabies shots in her belly. She had never forgotten the face of the wicked nurse at the village health clinic when she pushed those angry-looking needles into her belly to give the shots. Now she had to feed and walk two dogs, which was the worst challenge, but she needed to do whatever it took to look out for herself and her family in Wushishi. She accepted the job and would come on Sunday to start. Later that evening, she returned to the house with Indira, introduced her to Clara, and told her that she had accepted the live-in nanny job in Lower Manhattan and would start on Sunday. She begged Clara to understand and not hold it against her because she had a family in Wushishi to take care of and was willing and ready to get out there and face any odds. She wanted Clara to be her supporter until she could find her feet. Clara was not happy because Ngozi had been assisting her with laundry, cooking, and cleaning her apartment. She was also trying to keep an eye on her so that she could ensure a repayment of the loan. Ngozi told her that she would start paying off the loan with some of the money she made until she could pass her nursing board examination and get a better paying job. Clara agreed to take her to the new place to start her job.

FINDING A JOB

Mr. and Mrs. Cohen welcomed Ngozi to their home and introduced her to the children, Josh and Hannah, and the dogs, Tiger and Bear. Ngozi was happy to be around children again. As for the dogs, she was very uncomfortable. She quickly learned from Mrs. Cohen how to do things in the house, get the children ready for bed, cook meals, and use the washing machine for laundry. Her room was in the basement. It had a bed and a table with good lighting but was cold. She liked it and decided that she would make it a home. Mrs. Cohen offered her more blankets, a reading lamp, a fan, and a small heater. She told her to hide the fan and heater from her husband because their use could increase their energy bill. That was why they did not use them. Ngozi was grateful and cleaned up the room, put out her books, and arranged her things. She placed her family picture on the table, and tears filled her eyes. What were they doing now? Did they eat today, and was her husband unhappy or angry with the children? She would not tell him that she had taken a nanny job because that would upset him. Chima's wife, a nanny in America—that was absurd. Chima would never understand life in the USA until he got to come over. Even Ngozi did not understand it, but she was determined to make it for the interest of her family.

The Cohen children were little bunches of joy for her. Taking care of them gave her something to do, and once they were off to school, she had other listed chores to do. Mrs. Cohen made a list every morning detailing when and how she was to do them. Ngozi followed them strictly to the letter. Once her chores were done, she would settle on her bed at the basement, read her Bible, pray, and read her nursing books, preparing for her board examination. Ngozi could not get along with Bear. She had never been a dog lover because she was bitten by one as a child in her village. She would never pass through a road if a dog was sighted walking through that road. Now she had to take the dogs out for a walk, feed them, and clean after them. This was the worst of all her chores. She was completely horrified by the dogs. Bear appeared to know that Ngozi was petrified by his presence and had no problems making it worse by continuously barking and growling at her anytime she attempted to take him out for a walk. She had to do it, so like every other thing, she was determined to do it well. To overcome her fears, she would sing church hymns to the dogs and pray over them, and the dogs would immediately be calm, stop barking, and walk with her. That became the practice, but as soon as they came home from the walk, she would feed them, let them outside, close the back door, and be done with it. When the children came back from school, she would open the back door, and the dogs would come into the house and play with them.

When she had received her first pay ($250), she asked for permission to go to church that Sunday so as to pay her tithes as well as send money to her family. That Sunday morning, she went to a church service, after which she had found a Western Union office and sent $200 to her family. The man at the Western Union office helped her make the phone call to her husband, give him the money transfer number, and instruct her husband on how to get the money from the local bank the next day. She spoke to her husband and children, and everyone was happy.

Ngozi worked with the Cohens for another three months and did not get any day off for that period. She was getting very tired and unhappy with staying at home day in and day out and decided that she would like to attend a church service the next Sunday.

She asked Mrs. Cohen for a day off so that she could go to church, go out to the mall, and do some shopping for her children with the hope that she could mail it to her friend Clara, who would be going home next month. She could also send money home through Clara and find out how she would apply for her board exams. Mrs. Cohen reluctantly agreed to give her a day off but emphasized that she needed to be back by six o'clock in the evening to do her chores. That was good, but Ngozi did not realize that bus services on weekends run on longer schedules than on weekdays, and that made her come home at 8:15 p.m. Her employer was angry and locked the front door, refusing her entry back into the house despite all her efforts and pleas to explain what had happened. Finally, she was allowed to enter the house at around nine o'clock, with a lot of admonishing and attitude, which made her cry like a baby.

She immediately made up her mind to leave and return to New York to Clara's house that night. She went to her room in the basement and called her friend in Maryland, who immediately contacted Clara, and arrangements were made for her to take the train to the Bronx, and Clara would pick her up as soon as she arrived. She packed up her bags, even as Mrs. Cohen was calling her to get the kids ready for bed, and she came up to the living room and broke the news that she was leaving immediately because she could no longer take their nasty and inhumane treatment. Her employers were surprised and tried to talk her into staying, but Ngozi's mind was made up, and she really was ready to go. She was threatened with being reported to immigration services for being an illegal immigrant, with the consequence of being deported, but she went out the door as fast as she could. The Cohens reminded her that she would not be paid, and that was not an issue at that time.

She was finally on her way back to Clara but had made up her mind that she was not going to stay with her but would relocate to Maryland to stay with her friend. At the end of three months, she took the Maryland Board of Nursing exam, passed her test, and got her license. Her friend assisted her in getting a job in a nursing home, and the facility filed for her green card, which would give her permanent resident status. Her life and that of her family were about to change, and Ngozi was prepared to give her best to whatever she would do to succeed as a nurse in the USA. She stayed in the nursing home for two years, got her permanent resident status, and applied for her family to join her in the USA. The loan was paid off sooner from a second job she had picked up after settling in her nursing home schedule. The Absolute Agency took the money but had never found her employment because she was no longer in New York. Ngozi got information from Indira that the sponsoring agency was fake and that most of the people who had connected those like her to them were part of a "ring" and benefited somehow from the money they had gotten from vulnerable immigrant nurses. It was very sad to believe that Clara was going to rip her off, but Ngozi was not going to pursue Clara because the documents she had submitted to the American Embassy in Wushishi made processing her own documents faster and more successful.

CHALLENGES FACING IMMIGRANT NURSES IN AMERICA

Ngozi decided after one year of working in long-term care to go into acute care hospital nursing since this was what she had practiced back home. Working at a nursing home was a different type of nursing. She felt that she was not learning anything and would not grow professionally if she continued to be in that setting. She applied at an acute care academic hospital in Maryland and was accepted, and her joy knew no bounds. When she went to the hospital for her interview, she was overwhelmed with the environment, how the nurses, doctors, and other health-care professionals were working together. She noted the professionalism in the air, and she went immediately to a chapel in the hospital and cried out to God to help her get a job here as she wanted to advance her professional career to the highest level. During the interview, the nurse manager was very kind, knowledgeable, and impressed with her performance. She took her around the unit and introduced her to the nursing staff and a few of the resident doctors in the unit at that time. It was a medical surgical unit, and Ngozi applied for the night shift, as advised by her friend.

When she got home, she called her husband and told him all that she had seen and how happy she would be if she got a job in that hospital. Her enthusiasm was so high that she was talking fast and trying to say everything at the same time, expecting her husband to be happy and excited with her, but Chima dropped a bombshell, asking if the pay was as good as what she made at the nursing home. He reminded her that her journey to the USA was not to build a professional career. It was to make money to support the family and make plans to bring them over. In the meantime, she should stay with her present job as it was assisting the family to live better and start making some investments as well. He reminded her that all her friends in the USA were buying properties, building beautiful homes, sending exotic cars to their husbands, and investing in big bank accounts for their family. She should not be carried away by a professional career and needed to make sure the money was good. Ngozi was dumbfounded by her husband's reaction, and she could not find any words to respond, but she promised Chima that as soon as she settled down in the new job, she would find a second and even a third job to meet her financial obligations to the family. This was a wakeup call for her, but Ngozi told herself that her husband meant well and that she needed to work more and more to make Chima and the children happy.

The hospital's human resources department called her and offered her the job, with a small difference in the money that the nursing home was paying her. She was disappointed but accepted the offer because she wanted to work in a hospital like that and declined to tell Chima how much she would be making, even though he persistently asked. He did not want her to lower the monthly money she sent home for her family upkeep as it had made life easier for them. For the past two years, she had been sending Chima a monthly allowance, which was sometimes challenging and occasionally left her with nothing after paying her bills. Ngozi had also managed to send some money to her parents and siblings when she could. Her sisters and friends back home were concerned about her marriage that Chima might be tempted to get another wife, because of being lonely and taking care of children, Ngozi should reconsider and come back. All the children had been placed in boarding schools and Ngozi was paying for it all with her sweat in the USA. She did not want to believe them because Chima had told her about his investing their money in stocks, bonds, and debentures, and she had to accept it as the truth because it was for the family's future.

During her stay in New York, Ngozi was able to go out sometimes and mix with other people, but she would often meet an unbelievable but real cultural shock. Some of the people were unfriendly, not interested in assisting you even if you asked for help. They rarely spoke to you or even offered you a ride, a drink, or food. When she saw homeless people with their signs, begging for alms, she could hardly believe her eyes. As wealthy as America was, they had homeless people. In her country, there were not a lot of homeless people because there was always a family to step in and take care of them. The people you met on buses and trains would not speak to you. Even when you greet them or tried to engage them in a conversation, they would not respond. Rather, they would move away from you to another seat. She was very lonely and would sit by herself for a two-to-three-hour ride. She had been raised to respect those older than her, but she was shocked to notice in the buses and trains that elderly folks were standing, while younger people were sitting. She got tired of giving up her seat for people she considered older than her, to the point that even some of them would refuse to take the seat, making her look stupid. In the city of Bronx, New York, in Clara's apartment complex, the elevators were so filthy, with all sorts of profanities written on the walls. She wondered if this was America, where civilization was supposed to be the best. Why did the people urinate and defecate in the elevators in their apartment complexes? She could not make it out. The filthiness of the environment she saw in the project houses in New York was unbelievable, and Ngozi was still to be convinced that this was the world of her dreams, America.

In Maryland, the environment in the apartment complexes was cleaner. Folks were more laid back and friendly, even though occasionally, you felt ignored or will receive a witty flash of teeth in the form of a smile. You did not hear a lot of curse words on the buses, and the trains to Washington DC were cleaner. Maryland was almost like the city she had lived in in her country in some ways.

Ngozi was a very devout Christian in her country. She was always in church on Sundays with her family and involved in many church activities—bible class, intercessory prayers, kids' ministry, and choir and seniors assistance. She chose a church close to her house and decided to go into full ministry in the church. The first day at church, she was shocked to note that most of the members were over the age of sixty years. The children were brought mostly by their grandparents. She wondered where the young and middle-aged people were on Sunday morning. The service lasted for only one hour. The hymns were sung with such low tunes and feeble voices that it felt more like a funeral, rather than a praise worship service on a Sunday morning. The pastor was looking at his watch most of the time, like he was on a time watch, and when the service lasted for more than five minutes, people got up to leave. Outside the church, she noted that there were cars lined up, picking the grandparents and their grandchildren up from the church. During her next visits to the church for service or bible class, she noticed that once she sat on the pew, everyone else, both old and young, stayed away from her until she was always the only one sitting on a whole pew. When the pastor asked the congregation to move around and greet one another, no one came to her except the pastor and his wife. She could not understand if she was not welcomed to the church or if she had done something wrong.

As she later came to understand, the middle-aged and younger people were out on Sunday morning playing golf, basketball, or football. Church was something they did at their very young or very old age, which was also challenging because America is always referred to as God's own country. How then do you reconcile the fact that the people are not in church like back home? Why did God choose them as His people and not her own people back home, who lived, breathe, ate, and drank church all their lives. How could people discriminate against her in church, God's house, when the Bible said that we should love one another as we are all God's creation and children? She was not going to give up on her belief and would continue to go to church whether they accepted her or not. She knew whom she believed in, praised, and worshipped. God is the one she looked up to and not the folks in church. Gradually, after a long time of her persistence in coming, sitting all by herself in the pew, some of the elderly folks would stop on their way to smile at her or compliment her for her singing voice. It simply appeared as if she had forced herself to be accepted, but she knew that she had accepted everyone and loved and respected them, as her Christian faith had always taught her.

TECHNOLOGY

In the hospital, everything was done on the computer—medications, physician orders, and documentations, even clocking in your attendance at work. The use of the computer was very challenging because Ngozi had never seen a computer, let alone used one. She knew that Chima had taken a class in computer use because his company was converting their manual system of banking to computerization. She did not pay any attention to that since no one had ever mentioned or thought about computer use in the hospital she had worked in back home. Everything was done on paper. In the nursing home she had worked in, they were doing everything on paper. She had been oriented like that and was very used to that and did well, but here in the acute care hospital, she was faced with doing all her work on the computer. She was so terrified that she felt it had been a mistake to switch to the hospital. She should have listened to her husband and stayed at the nursing home. She confided in her preceptor that she did not know how to use the computer, and she advised her to go to the human resources office and inquire about taking a class. She was grateful and proceeded to human resources and registered to take a class on weekends. As a result, she had to quit her weekend work at the nursing home, making it impossible to make enough money to pay her bills and send the required monthly stipend to her family. She was scared of how disappointed her husband would be and what challenges he would be facing in taking care of the family if she could not afford to send money, but she had to take this computer class. Ngozi was determined and did all she could to learn how to use the computer to keep this new job. The computer instructor noted her anxiety and worry about not picking up the skills quickly, decided to loan her one of the computers (desktop) to use for practice at home, and even took a step to visit her house to ensure that she got Wi-Fi and had the desktop set. By the end of the first two weeks of class, Ngozi was able to type on the keyboard and understand the differences in Word documents, Excel spreadsheets, and other features required for basic concepts in using a computer. She continued with her nursing unit orientation. Her preceptor was very understanding and took extra steps to assist her with her documentation. She would swipe out at the end of her shift and stay an extra one to two hours to get her documentation and work done on the computer before going home. Most days, she got home by nine in the morning from a seven o'clock night shift.

Some of the staff were talking about her as if she were dumb or did not "get it." They were quick to point out her honest mistakes, write her up, or report her to the nurse manager. As a result, she got some corrective action for time management skills. In the midst of this, she felt all alone and no longer had time to hang out with her friends as before. Some of these friends were telling her that it was a mistake transferring to the hospital setting. She should have stayed in the nursing home like they did and be relieved from all the demands of acute care nursing. They told her that her license was in jeopardy if she continued to make mistakes or that she may be sued if any of her mistakes impacted a patient negatively. Ngozi did not give up. She was her father's daughter. He had instructed them as children to remain focused, and they would succeed. This challenge rekindled that fire in her that she had used when they relocated to the city and when she was faced with a challenging new school environment. She had left her family for one thing, to succeed, and she understood that the road was not going to be rosy or without challenges. She continued to pray and fast, asking God to be her strength and guide her in her lonely quest to assist her family.

The next challenge was the use of electronic pumps for the intravenous administration of fluids and medications in the hospital, cardiac telemetry monitoring, monitoring patients on chronic ventilators, and complex procedures such as peritoneal dialysis. There were some other electronic gadgets and equipment used for patient care in the acute care hospital that Ngozi had no idea how to use. She was not used to using electronic gadgets back home, and some of them were only used in specialty areas in her home country. She had a lot to learn, but with some of her colleagues already talking about her, she was scared to even ask questions or admit her lack of knowledge and skills. She summoned the courage one day and talked to her nurse manager, the unit clinical educator, and the director of professional practice department. It was an uphill task to do that because she was not sure how she would be received, but it was better to speak up than to wallow around in ignorance and cause a negative outcome for a patient. Even though she was still on orientation, she did not trust that her preceptors would be as helpful as she needed because she had actually been hired as coming with "experience." Her manager and the unit clinical educator had a meeting with her to evaluate her needs, and the manager decided to transfer her to the day shift for six months to assist her with more support and opportunities to learn the skills required in her practice. It was a thoughtful and meaningful move because there were so many people on the day shift who were willing to assist and mentor her while she continued to practice her computer skills at home.

This change of shift resulted in a reduction in her incomes she has to lose the night differential pay, but she had to make up for that by returning to the nursing home on weekends to pick up some shifts. She made only enough to send money home, pay her bills, and purchase gas for her car. No personal needs were met, not even to pay her tithes in church, and this was making her sad, but she could not tell Chima that there was a need to reduce the amount of monthly money sent home, even temporarily. Her husband would not understand, and she was not ready to get into a fight from millions of miles away. She had to do everything she could to support her family, and as long they were happy, she was okay. Things were not getting better back home, as she was always made to understand and hear from the news and people she communicated with.

Patients and Their Families

The patients and their families were another area of challenge. In her country, the patients and their families were very respectful, even fearful of making the nurses and doctors angry. They hardly questioned your skills or knowledge and were grateful when you did anything for them. The patients' families were always around and assisted in providing care for their loved ones, such as bathing, feeding, bringing meals, making beds, and transporting them to test areas. All throughout her practice in her country, she had never seen a patient fall or have any skin or mobility issues because the family members were present, ready, and willing to learn how to assist the patient. This involvement of the family in the provision of care for loved ones in hospitals in her country resulted from the fact that the health-care system in her country was not operated with health insurance coverage. The patient and their family paid out of their pocket, so they did all they could to get their family member out of the hospital early to avoid huge hospital bills if possible.

Ngozi learned about the "almighty patient rights," which sometimes transcended to situations or incidences where the care provider was being treated with disrespect, disregard, and disdain.

She was shocked at how many times the patient called the nurse for one thing or another, even with the family members sitting around the bedside. She also noted that the family members most times asked you questions as if you were an enemy or you came to work with the aim or goal of making their loved one sicker. Most times, she would go to the bathroom and cry because of how a family member or patient had talked down to her. Some would ask questions like "How did you come to America?" with some form of ridicule. She could not understand why they were quick to report you to your boss, even when you did not respond to all the bashing, lashing out, cursing, and humiliation you were subjected to just from being a nurse assigned to take care of the patient. The manager told her that it was her "nonverbal communication" (body language) that had made the patient upset and resulted in customer dissatisfaction. Body language, what does that mean? She did not respond, but had stood in the room until the cursing and bashing for no slightest provocation ended. How does the body speak ,and in what language. On a particular day, she was taking care of a young adult female patient who was admitted for a sickle cell crisis and was being transfused with blood. The patient was also on a patient-controlled analgesia (PCA) pump with a strong narcotic—hydromorphone (Dilaudid) for pain management. The patient put on her call light every ten to fifteen minutes, asking for the doctor to be called to increase the dose and rate of her pain medication in the pump. Ngozi called the doctor six times within the hour until the doctor yelled at her, asking her to use her nursing judgment, if she had any.

The doctor remarked rudely, "Which part of the world jungle did you get your nursing training? They bring you people from the jungle to take care of patients, knowing that you have no single iota of nursing judgment. Do not call me again."

Ngozi became demoralized, and the patient kept asking for more medication. She could not handle the issue, so she asked the charge nurse to reassign the patient to another nurse. The charge nurse told her that the assignment had been made. She needed to explain to her patient that she could not continue to ask for pain medication but to use her pump. The patient's mother arrived and called for the nurse. When Ngozi came in, she started yelling at her with all forms of profanity and asked for the charge nurse or manager because Ngozi did not know what she was doing and should no longer be the nurse for her daughter. The patient was screaming at the top of her voice that her pain was worse than ever before and that she needed to speak to the hospital CEO. There was chaos on the unit, and everyone was looking at her like she had done something wrong. The night supervisor was called, and she spoke with the patient and her family and asked the charge nurse to reassign the patient to another nurse and write up Ngozi for poor performance.

The next morning, the nurse manager took her to her office and questioned her on what had happened at night. Ngozi could not speak a word. She was sobbing as if she had lost a loved one, and her whole body was shaking, so the manager asked her to go home, take that night off, and write up what the problem was. She went home and decided to open up to one of her friends about the challenges and ordeals she had been going through in the hospital. Both of them decided to speak to a lawyer, who proceeded to write her own side of the story and, at the same time, highlighted some of the challenges and problems (scheduling, patient assignments, and bullying) she had been subjected to in the workplace. She paid $300 for the letter, which not only was addressed to her nurse manager but also copied the human resources and chief nursing officer (CNO) of the hospital. Although she had submitted the letter, she was petrified and was waiting for a letter that would terminate her employment. On the contrary, the letter created some awareness and made the CNO investigate some the challenges faced by immigrant nurses, and a committee was put together to take responsibility in monitoring, mentoring, and integrating the immigrant nurses in the hospital. Ngozi came to realize that the executive nursing leadership were not aware of the burden and challenges faced by immigrant nurses who were hired in the hospitals, especially if they had come on their own and not through the contracted hospital foreign hiring agency.

COMMUNICATION

Not all immigrant nurses speak English fluently, and that was the reason why the Immigration and Naturalization Services (INS) required immigrating nurses to take some English tests—the TOEFL and the TSE. These tests were part of the requirement prior to taking the National Council Licensure Examination for Registered Nurses (NCLEX-RN) and the board exam as well as obtaining the H-1B visa that eventually granted you permanent resident status from employment. Ngozi did not have any spoken or written English language problem. All her education was done in the English language, and because her country had been colonized by the British, English was the lingua franca. She actually prided herself on speaking the Queen's English, but America had their own English language, and the hospital had its own form of communication pattern that bordered on acronyms, mnemonics, short phrases, and abbreviations. This was challenging to her as she had to ask questions for the explanation of some terms. She went to a thrift store and bought an American dictionary, but it was not very helpful. She used a lot of online encyclopedias and Google search, and this impacted her time management. Ngozi resorted to using these resources because she had been humiliated enough for asking genuine, relevant patient-related questions, and instead of making mistakes, she would rather take the long process of finding out for herself. She kept a log of words, phrases, abbreviations, and acronyms. The pocketbook became her brain and companion everywhere. Her stress level was at its highest point, and her blood pressure, heart rate, and whole body were reacting in one way or another to the challenges.

When she was working in the nursing home at the beginning of her U.S. employment life, there was a young resident (patient) who was physically disabled, mentally challenged, and on her preceptor's assignment for the shift. The resident was always loud and disruptive and yelled at the top of his voice. In fact, he was kept at the end of the unit to ensure that he did not wake up all the elderly residents or scare them with his screams. He used curse words, and every sentence he uttered began and ended with the f-word. Ngozi had never heard a curse word before, not to talk about the f-word. Her preceptor asked her to go and give the resident some ginger ale, which was what he had been screaming out for. Ngozi went to the room with two cans of ginger ale. The resident screamed out more at the sight of the ginger ale and demanded some "f——ing water." He yelled it out so loudly, and she had to run out of the room.

She went to her preceptor, who was on break with other staff in the break room, and innocently asked, "I'm not sure he wants the ginger ale. Where can I find the f——ing water to give to him?"

Everyone turned toward her and burst out with laughter, and shouts of "Oh my god!" filled the room, and she was totally taken aback.

She kept saying, "That is what the resident is asking for, and it is not in the refrigerator."

The laughter stopped, and they explained to her that there was no such water, but she needed to know that this was a curse word, and that resident would always say that before whatever he was asking for. Lesson one: learned about curse words and their use. In the hospital, during the night shift, she took a report one night from an off-going nurse who said, "The patient in room 2311 is a frequent flyer, just FYI."

Ngozi went in to introduce herself to her patient, and after exchanging pleasantries, she asked the patient, "I understand that you are a frequent flyer. Which airline do you fly?"

The real English (British) use of the term *frequent flyer* relates to airlines. She did not understand that it was a term that is commonly used to describe a patient who is frequently readmitted. The patient was very upset and reported her to the charge nurse, who calmed the patient down. She understood that it was an honest statement borne out of ignorance and a lack of understanding of what the term meant. Lesson two: learned about the use of phrases.

When she communicated with a colleague, patient, or family member, they always asked her to repeat herself because they did not understand her. One day she summoned the courage to ask another nurse if she understood English because she was communicating in the English language.

The nurse laughed and stated, "I understand English, but I do not understand you because you have an accent."

Ngozi went back to her friend and asked her what *accent* meant, but she could not explain except that it is a word coined in America to remind you, "You are from another part of the world, and we have no time to be patient and understand what you are saying." Ngozi tried to imitate her colleagues by speaking slightly through her nose to make her sound like them and speak faster than usual like them. It worked, and she was on the road for her communication to be accepted, although it continued to be challenging, even when she spoke slowly and repeated herself many times.

Peer-to-Peer Relationship

Ngozi could not, for sure, understand why each time she was on duty, she got all the challenging total-care patients, the ones with high acuity or challenging, mean, and demanding families. She would always be assigned to work with the nursing assistant, who would not assist you in doing anything for the patients nor answer their call lights or even perform their own assigned duties. These nursing assistants were the ones who would quickly tell you that they were the "grandmothers of the unit," had been there since the unit was opened, and had no problem ganging up on you. It appeared most of the RNs either were afraid of them or had to buy dinner for them to get their cooperation. Ngozi did not have the resources to buy dinner or presents for anyone, so she resorted to not asking for their assistance and would do everything for her patients, while the nursing assistants stayed on their computers, their cell phones, or the breakroom all night. Sometimes she wondered if the nurse manager was aware of this practice at night, but she could not say anything for fear of retaliation. The weight of the job, environment, and lack of support were taking a huge toll on her life and personality. She hung onto the knowledge that she had come to the USA to seek a better future for her family, and nothing was going to be in her way. She was going to keep doing her best, knowing that God would see her through. She intensified her prayers, and the Serenity Prayer became her watchword every time she was faced with one challenge or another.

Some of her peers (RNs) were kind to her and would assist her from time to time, while others were just ignoring and bullying her in one way or another. She assisted them whenever she could and was going to show love and kindness to all of her team. She was never involved in anything that was going on in the unit—from birthday celebrations, baby showers, and bridal showers up to the communal ordering of food from the Chinese restaurant at the start of the shift. She brought her food always and used the microwave in the break room to warm it because she did not wish to order any meals from outside as every cent meant a lot for her family. One night she warmed up her food and was eating during her break in the break room when one of the obnoxious nursing assistants came into the room and started to make faces at her. She did not pay any attention to her until she asked Ngozi what kind of food she had warmed up that "stunk" up the whole room. Ngozi innocently answered that it was rice with fish stew and vegetables. The nursing assistant told her that she should not warm such food in the unit's break room but take it to the cafeteria on the ground floor. She should spare them "the smell of her nasty food." Ngozi immediately stopped eating, turned around to the nursing assistant as she was about to leave the room, and warned her that she should never talk to her again in such a manner, or else she would report her to the nurse manager. Ngozi told her that she was very rude and insulting and that she would no longer tolerate foolish acts from her nor any other person. She educated her fiercely on being professional, courteous, and respectful. The boldness of never giving up or allowing anyone to disrespect her in any manner, which her grandmother and parents had instilled in her, came flying out. Ngozi was ready to pounce on the girl, but she remembered that there was a reason for her being in this place and country (her family) and held herself. Ngozi was so infuriated that she was almost going to throw the bowl of rice on her, but another nursing assistant entered the room and inquired as to what was going on because they were loud. Ngozi told her all that had happened, and the nursing assistant decided to report to the charge nurse and shift director. Everyone condemned the act of the nursing assistant, and it was agreed that all the RNs would wait in the morning to talk to their manager. It was a very humiliating and depressing moment for Ngozi, but once again, she recited the Serenity Prayer to herself, and the shift continued. This event would never be forgotten because this was a price too high to pay for family and profession.

Education and Career Advancement

Ngozi knew that for her to advance her career, she would have to obtain bachelor's and master's degrees in nursing, but the thought of paying school fees, assisting her children through school, and maintaining her household and family in Wushishi stared her in the face. She had always been a determined person, and her faith that with God, all things were possible was strong. She decided to ask her friends and colleagues on how to get around this feat, but they did not give the best advice. Some of them thought that she was very ambitious and that as an immigrant, her dreams of advancing her career were not reachable. There was no place in nursing leadership for immigrant nurses. Ngozi refused to be daunted but continued to research for the best possible means to obtain a higher nursing education without putting her family in distress. She reluctantly discussed the plans with her husband, who surprisingly became supportive but would not provide any financial assistance, even though paying some bills. Chima was also struggling. He did not get a good job or a job in the banking industry that matched his position or career in his country. He decided to pick up a job as a stocking person in Giant Food Stores. It brought in some income but was not enough to pay for anything (bills) significant in the house. It was also depressing and humiliating for him to work so hard, stocking wares in the store, with supervisors shouting and screaming at him to move faster.

Ngozi decided to enroll in an online program for a BSN and MSN and proceeded to take a school loan while she struggled and juggled three jobs to meet her family's financial obligations. In five years, Ngozi graduated with a master's degree in nursing and proceeded to apply for career advancement in her job when a nurse manager position opened in one of the units she had worked in earlier. It was not an easy feat. Her spirit was willing, even when her body was weak. Her initial application was rejected, and no reason was provided, but she refused to be discouraged or believe that her being a migrant (foreign-born citizen) was the reason. She continued to improve herself through education, nursing certifications, conferences, participation in nursing research, and process improvement projects, with the goal of advancing her career in nursing leadership. She could not continue to work at the patient's bedside because she was tired, burnt out, and frustrated. Believing that she had acquired enough experience, education, leadership skills, and knowledge required to be a nurse leader, she continued to apply for open positions in her facility and other hospitals, but where was the opportunity that had always been brandished around about diversity, equal opportunity, and nondiscrimination in employment? Would she ever get her dream fulfilled in the land of opportunities and the "big American dream"? Does being an immigrant nurse constitute a hindrance or barrier to career advancement, as her friends had advised? Was this why most of her immigrant nurse colleagues refused to do any other thing than bedside nursing? Could this be the reason that most of them resorted to being charge nurses and did nothing else? She had come to America to fulfill a lot of dreams, one of them being career advancement, so what was the reason for not achieving her goals, even after getting the education, experience, knowledge, and skills required for all these years? Ngozi noted that some of her nonimmigrant colleagues seemed to get leadership positions even when she knew that she was more qualified, but something seemed to be against her advancing, and she could not get her thoughts around what it was. Hopefully, it was not because she was an immigrant nurse in America. Despite all the challenges that Ngozi had faced as an immigrant nurse in the USA, it came to a time where she has to evaluate the success or failure of her migration. She decided to do this by reviewing it along with the *Merriam-Webster Dictionary*'s definitions of *success* and *failure*. *Success* is defined as the accomplishment of an aim or purpose. *Failure*, on the other hand, is defined as the lack of success.

In the earlier chapters, I narrated why Ngozi and Chima decided for her to migrate to the USA: family safety and welfare, financial stability, improved living conditions, good educational opportunities, job satisfaction and stability, career advancement, and a future for her children in the world. Looking back, Ngozi has cause to be grateful for her migration because she has success stories, but at the same time, there were lots of instances and occasions that had her witness failure in her goals and aspirations.

Some of the success stories that she recounts include educational opportunities for her and her children. She was able to obtain a BSN and MSN in her career. Her children were able to obtain first and second college degrees, which enabled them to get good jobs in various areas of life. Her family had been exposed to the competition that exists in the USA, and they were able to favorably compete and be successfully rewarded for their work.

Ngozi's children came to learn that hard work ensures success, and they worked hard in anything they did to achieve success. They did not forget their roots and family in their country of origin and kept their childhood friends, cousins, nephews, and uncles and aunties. On many occasions, they would seek donations from colleagues and friends for items such as clothes, books, shoes, food, medications, and money to send home to their families and community. They traveled occasionally to visit their families and friends back in Wushishi and organize activities such as school sports competitions and educational and Bible quizzes with gifts for the children in the community. They organized a roving library with books donated by their friends and organizations here in the USA.

They offered scholarships for eligible children in the villages to pay for high school education, medical and educational short term mission trips, partnering with U.S. nonprofit organizations and churches. Their quest to give back extended to many countries they could participate and reach out to. Ngozi became successful in her career and was promoted to a middle-level leadership position in her workplace. She had opportunities to attend big nursing conferences and participated in a speaker's forum for nursing best practice discussions. Ngozi had done presentations related to evidence-based practices in projects at her job and school. She was honored with recognition awards within her facility and outside for her educational professional and career achievements. Some of her works were published on national journals, and that was all part of her dream.

As a born-again Christian, Ngozi realized and understood that biblical success is different from the dictionary's definition of *success*. She wanted to review if she had really attained success in the Christian biblical sense. The Bible has always given us a strong difference from the misguided worldly definition, which, at the end, summarizes *success* as the ability to work hard and be anything we can be in this world. The scriptures, through Jesus's parable of the talents (Matthew 25:14–30 KSV), teach us differently and give us five great meanings of success. Success is a product of our work, as seen in Genesis, when God commanded Adam to work by stewarding and growing the resources given to him. In this way, we are all mandated to be good stewards of all that we have been given wherever we find ourselves until Christ's return. Second, success is realizing that God gives us everything we need to do what he has called us to do, to invest like the servant in the parable wisely toward a productive end. We need to know that we work for the master, not our own selfish purposes, and one day we will be held accountable for our actions.

Ngozi always defined her successes within the scriptural mindset and would not conclude categorically that her migration was successful. She had her dreams fulfilled of not only becoming a nurse but also fulfilling her biblical understanding of working for God so as to use her work (talents) to fulfill her earthly calling. She got involved in short term medical missions trips to third world countries with her friends, colleagues, and church. During these trips, they were able to perform health screenings as well as education and promotion programs using resources donated from organizations, families, and friends in the USA. They were able to network with nurses in other parts of the world through combined seminars, the sharing of ideas, knowledge, and skills, and the donation of nursing books, journals, materials, and equipment. Ngozi's mission field included some local work within her church, community, and neighborhood. She does not yet claim success per the scriptures but does continue to view her immigration as a race set before her that she will continue to run with the hope that God wants her to have in Christ. When that race is done, she can count her success in the prize won. Ngozi and her family have recorded some failures that bring some sad moments and that feeling of the incompleteness of life. As a migrant nurse, she has, so many times, had the feeling of isolation and being unacceptable in the community and country she calls her own. She has always wondered why some of her colleagues and patients, even the folks she has met in the community, ask, whether with good intentions or not, if she will ever return to her "country of origin." This question has always reminded her that irrespective of having attained citizenship status in the USA, she is still considered a foreigner, no matter how much she puts into the system to which she has given everything she could all these years. Not being totally accepted and integrated in the country to which she has dedicated her life, career, and obedience draws tears to her eyes on many occasions. She does not understand why that question comes up from even the very patients she has taken responsibility for in their time of fragility and need. Sometimes the patients or families will ask, "You have an accent. Where did you originally come from?" or say, "Let me place or guess your origin from your accent." These questions are never asked of some colleagues from Canada, Texas, England, and Scotland, who naturally have deep accents as well. Why she and other immigrant nurses are being asked this question always is concerning and troubling, to say the least. This act goes to prove that there exists a lack of acceptance and integration of immigrants even after so many years of immigration history.

Another area of failure is on the issue of career advancement. Although Ngozi was promoted to a middle-level manager in her facility, she has always felt that there is unspoken and hidden discrimination when it comes to promotions, career advancement, and recognitions. She believes that as a migrant nurse, you have to double your efforts to get recognized or promoted to a higher level of leadership in the nursing career. In one of the hospitals where she had worked, she believed that she was adequately prepared and qualified for an open leadership position, and she applied. She was denied the position with little or no reason, but later, she found out it was because she was an immigrant nurse. It does not matter if you have all the degrees, certifications, experience, etc. required for a position. The simplest excuse can make you fail to advance. In most institutions, it is noted that the executive nursing leadership has 0–1 percent of migrant nurses in the top level positions, even though most migrant nurses have good education, skills, and knowledge to be in such positions. All the talk about diversity and inclusion ends in the meeting rooms and is not actualized. Ngozi feels this especially when she knows that many migrant nurses possess all the relevant and required credentials to be in executive leadership, but the system consistently fails to absorb them.

Another area of failure is missing out on family events in her home country of Wushishi. Ngozi has missed out on some important family events: marriages, funerals, initiations, and title-taking ceremonies. Most of these events are the cultural norms and festivities she enjoyed with her family, relations, and friends. She missed most of them because she could not afford to travel back home every time there was an event. Most of these events happened during the holidays, such as the Christmas and New Year seasons, but most hospital policies do not allow employees to take vacations from December 15 to January 3. Most organizations will be reluctant to allow vacation times of more than three weeks, especially during major holidays. Any time off for less than a month will not be sufficient for Ngozi to travel to her home country and enjoy being with her family and relations before heading back. She was not there when her parents, aunts, and uncles had died. She could not get to them on time during their illness, which was one of her reasons for becoming a nurse, but she could not provide such nursing care for them when they were sick and needed her. She had even heard that her parents did not get good care in the hospital when they were ill and that the nurses had treated them with rudeness and contempt. That hurt her so badly. Most of her relatives and village folks whom she had grown up with died from simple ailments that could have been prevented through health education and promotion. When Ngozi hears about any of her family members dying, it is usually a bad day for her. She feels guilty for the fact that she betrayed them. She was the first nurse from her village. They were all proud and supportive and looked forward to the day and time their own daughter would be working side by side with the doctors in the local hospital taking care of them. They were so proud of her becoming a nurse that it was announced at the local church service after her graduation from nursing school. Her parents and the entire village celebrated her success with feasting and dancing. She was already regarded as the "doctor" because they believed that she was very smart and outspoken and would even do better that any of the white missionary nurses working in the local hospital. All their hopes were dashed to the ground when she left the village to go to the city for a job, but she was still coming home on some weekends to conduct some health screenings and hold education and promotion programs. She was always teaching them how to manage infantile convulsions, fevers, and diarrhea. She would always give health talks about the prevention of malaria in the village by just keeping the environment free of things that can create room for mosquitos breeding. All that stopped as she migrated to the USA, and most of her relatives died from preventable illnesses.

Ngozi missed all her friends because she was no longer in their circles as before. Occasionally, when she returned to visit, she found out that most of them had also migrated, retired to the villages, or even died. The ones left in the city were not as friendly as before, and she could not understand why. They saw her as someone superior or whom they were no longer friends with. It did not matter how much she tried to do the same things they had all done together. She still felt like an outsider. That is a huge failure, when you can no longer be together freely with your childhood friends as much as you would want to, not because of any fault of yours but because of a complex created by distance and being apart for a while, pursuing personal dreams and no longer the collective dream you all shared together as children.

Another failure that is noted by immigrant nurses is the clash of culture for their families, especially the children. Ngozi's children came to the USA in their adolescent years, and within a couple of months, the environment and society were creeping in to change their outlook on life. In school, they were faced with the challenge of being accepted by their peers without getting into gangs, drugs, or anything that was considered bad behavior. Every day these children come home to face parents who want them to focus on their studies, not join any groups or try to make friends because the school environment can sometimes be dangerous and most of the kids in school were bad influences. Sometimes her children did not want to approach their peers to ask for assistance with schoolwork, which was one way kids back home learned and developed with one another freely. Ngozi had to get her children enrolled in private after-school programs that offered assistance with homework and classwork but at a very expensive price. Ngozi could not afford a lot of sessions, but her children used every opportunity they had and studied among themselves, assisting one another. They learned how to use the library and work together to solve their schoolwork. Sometimes Ngozi worked extra hours to pay for private classes in her home to assist her children in coping with this new educational system.

NEIGHBORHOOD

Ngozi and her children came from an environment where children and their families were each other's keepers. Talk about the theme "It takes a village to raise a child." That was explicit in what her home environment portrayed. Here in the USA, they hardly knew who their next-door neighbor was nor were able to play safely with the children in the neighborhood. Everyone stays in their homes, and people rarely relate or talk to each other for fear of interfering or being "nosy." In her country of origin, the word *nosy* means "concern," a positive thing, not negative. Everyone knows everyone and can take care of you and your children until you return from work or the market. On few occasions, when Ngozi's children had tried to play or reach out to the children in her neighborhood, they were mistreated, called names, threatened, and ganged up on. They retreated to staying indoors, watching TV, and playing with one another. In one way, it made them become closer and always stick together. Most migrant nurses have the same stories as Ngozi, and in the next chapter, you will hear some of their stories.

Voices of Immigrant Nurses

The questions below were put out to some nurses from other countries who had migrated to the USA. Most of those selected for these interviews were what I called first-generation migrant nurses. In other words, they were practicing nurses in their countries of origin before coming to the USA. Other nurses interviewed were those I chose to call second-generation migrant nurses. In other words, their mothers were first-generation nurse migrants, and they became nurses as well. I also interviewed American nurses who had worked with the migrant nurses to hear their own experiences with them and how they had assisted them through their journeys. These are some of the questions in the interview. Each of the respondents was asked the same questions.

Name:
Age:
Area of Practice:
Specialty:

Q1.   Where you from, and what are brought you to the USA?

Q2.   How long have you been a nurse, and did you practice nursing in your country? If so, for how long?

Q3.   What challenges did you face during your transition to the USA, and how did you overcome them?

Q4.   What kind of support systems did you have during your challenging transition to the USA?

Q5.   Do you still face challenges as a result of being an immigrant nurse in the USA?

Q6.   Would you consider your migration a success or a failure? Why?

Nurse #1

My name is Zeeman, A. M., fifty-nine years old, in rehabilitation nursing. I am from Ethiopia, and came to the USA for a better life. This year is my thirty-eighth year of being a nurse, I was a nurse anesthetist in my country for eighteen years. At the beginning, it was not easy until I passed the boards here in the USA. I worked as a babysitter and housekeeper and then became a certified nursing assistant (CNA) in the same hospital where I currently work as an RN after passing my board licensing exam. I did not have any support system for my transition. Most of the people I knew back home were living in New York, but I arrived at the country and settled in Maryland. I was very lonely, felt lost, and had no one to really look up to or reach out to. Eventually, I summoned the courage and found a church where I met some Ethiopians, and they quickly became my family. From that time on, I had resources and got a job as a babysitter/housekeeper. As I made some money, I registered in a CNA program and graduated as a nursing assistant. I applied for a job at my present workplace and started working as a can, and that was how I got here. Then I passed the boards and was hired as an RN. My professional career commenced and brought some fulfillment. Some of the challenges I had encountered on my journey included getting used to the nursing practice here in the USA because it is quite different from that in my country. Communication was a challenge and still is a challenge for me today. English is not my primary language, and sometimes I cannot speak it clearly. I chose to work the night shift because it is not so much talking to colleagues or patients/families but more of doing nursing tasks, keeping patients safe, and ensuring that they have no issues. During the day, there are so many activities that require the nurse to communicate more, and I was not sure if I could do that easily and well. I took some spoken English classes, which have assisted in improving my communication to the point where it is right now. Presently, I do not have any more challenges that are tied to my being an immigrant nurse. Things have become better than before, but it is still a daily struggle.

My migration is a success because I live a better life here than back home and am able to help my family back home better than when I was in my country. I have no regrets except that I still have to plan what to do after retirement. I am not sure whether to remain here in the USA or return to Ethiopia.

Nurse #2

My name is Fatmata Sheku, forty-five years old. I am originally from Sierra Leone but migrated from London (Brent) to join my ex-husband. We migrated to the USA through the DV lottery visa. In my country of origin, I was not a nurse but worked as a private secretary in the local government of my district. When I had joined my hospital in London, I enrolled in the UK nursing program to become a licensed nurse. After my education, I got hired and worked in a community hospital medical surgical unit for six years. During my period in England, I did not witness or face any challenges because my education, training, and clinical rotations were in the same hospital I had applied to work in as an RN. There were some small elements of frustration occasionally, not challenges as an immigrant but mostly those as a new nurse, but I was able to cope and improve my performance as the years rolled by and was promoted to assistant nurse manager prior to my coming to the USA. I enjoyed every bit of my life as a nurse, even up until now. In London, we did a lot of team nursing. As you know, that was the British practice model then. I am not sure what they are using now, but even with the team nursing model, a huge multidisciplinary practice was very evident. It was less stressful because everyone's opinion was taken into consideration for the patient care plan and practice. When I migrated to the USA, it took me two years before I passed my nursing board exam to get a license. I took NCLEX review classes, especially after my first failed attempt at the board examination. Quickly, I realized that to pass the board licensing exam, I had to jettison my London nursing ideas and study the practice of nursing in the USA. The critical thinking part of the nursing practice was completely different and very challenging to me, related to the practice and culture of the American people. During the time of waiting to get my RN license, I enrolled in the CNA program, passed, and was hired as a private-duty CNA with a home health agency. In the meantime, my ex-husband was the sole breadwinner. All the regular household bills (babysitters, food, rent, car payments) were on him, and it caused a lot of stress at home than love. The private-duty CNA job provided an opportunity for me to earn some money, work around my children's programs, and study for my licensing exams. It was rough, to say the least, and my marriage was falling apart.

Finally, when I obtained my nursing license, job opportunities opened up for me, and I got a job in a nursing home, where I worked for two years, and later transferred to an acute rehabilitation hospital. The transition was very challenging for me as an RN. At work, during my recruitment interviews, my six years of experience as a nurse in London were never taken into consideration for the job offers. Some of the hospitals I had applied to initially rejected my application for "lack of experience." I trained in London, not in Kitwe. It was very disappointing and demoralizing, but when I worked in the nursing home for six months, that was considered "USA experience." The nursing work environment was not friendly, the licensed practical nurse (LPN) and CNAs were consistently a challenge. They were defiant and would decline taking delegations from me for resident care. I was so intimidated to the point that most times, it was easier and less stressful to provide care to the resident by myself, while all my colleagues sat at the nurse's station, chatting away. When I asked for assistance, I got pushbacks because the LPN was my charge nurse and supervisor. They made fun of me sometimes, as if I did not know what to do. I was almost losing confidence in my nursing practice and judgment. That was why I decided to go back to the hospital.

My marriage was on the rocks because of stress. We eventually ended up divorcing as we could no longer be together. That was another challenge, managing two young children as a single mom. I could never balance my work with my life. I relocated to another state to start my life again with my kids and had to bring my mother to assist me with the children. My migration has both successes and failures. My success in my nursing career can be attributed to my relocation, my mother coming over to assist, and my decision to start my life again. In the new state, I had no problems getting my license through the compact state RN licensure benefits. The nurse manager who had hired me at her unit in the rehabilitation hospital became my mentor. She was a very kind, compassionate person and gave me every opportunity to help my practice grow gradually. She corrected my mistakes with respect and such openness that I understood it was for the patient's safety and care. I later got to know that she was also a migrant nurse from England like me, so we became friends. My mother's presence was very helpful and supportive for me and my children. I had the opportunity to work more than one job to pay all the debts that we had incurred from schools and other necessities of life in America for a single mom living her dream. My nursing career is going well. I have gotten my bachelor's in nursing and wish to pursue a master's in nursing administration. My mother has gotten permanent resident status and will file for my siblings in Sierra Leone to come over here for education and life changes. My children are doing well in school and moving ahead in their various careers. We have integrated well into the community, made friends, and found families from Sierra Leone to bond with.

One of my greatest failures is my divorce because both my husband and I bulked under the pressures and stress of the USA, which we did not experience in London. We purchased a country flat in London, with our early savings, but lost it to the foreclosure company. The tenants who had rented it after we left could not pay the mortgage as it was due. That was a huge economic loss for all the family savings from my marriage. The irony of it all is the relationship that had made me leave my country of origin is gone for no other reason than our second migration. Losing it is a huge regret and failure for me, especially as my children are growing up without a strong father figure. I would not give up on this if my journey were to start from the beginning again, but I guess it's all over as my ex-husband returned to Sierra Leone and got himself another wife and children. I wish him luck and am moving on.

Nurse #3

My name is Indira. I am sixty-two years old from India. I have been a nurse for thirty-six years and practiced in the medical surgical nurse specialty. I practiced for three years in India, migrated to Wushishi with my husband for two years, and then migrated to the USA. We came to the USA to look for a better opportunity for my family. As soon as we got here, I started preparing for my licensure board exam to get a job. My husband started working in a fast food restaurant and took on other odd jobs to support us (me and my children). We were supported more by my aunt, who offered us accommodations, food, money, and all that made life easier for us. We had some cultural shock related to communication, community, and getting our immigration status updated. Eventually, I passed the State boards and got a hospital job that opened the door for my getting a H-1B visa. As time progressed, we got our work permits and green cards. Then we moved from my aunt's place to find our place for a total of two years.

In my nursing practice, I had challenges with the equipment, technology, and communication with the other providers and even some of my peers. I was lucky to have some Indian nurses who were already working in the hospital where I was employed, and they became my resources and mentors. That was a huge source of support for me. Also, the food was expensive as we could not really appreciate or tolerate American cuisine, so it was hard to manage our grocery list, pay for our rent and car, and purchase clothes with the small money we were bringing home. But the children understood that they could not have more than we could afford, and that set their lifestyle of being content and thrifty with money, even until today. Presently, my challenge is that I am getting older and have all these health issues that come with aging, but I am still grateful to have migrated to the USA. I will state that my migration is a huge success because if I was still back in India or Wushishi, I would have been retired from working by now. Here in the USA, even though there is a stipulated retirement age, you can still work if you are able and continue to make money to improve your life. My children were able to get their education in their chosen careers and become successfully employed. The only failure I can think of is that I have lost touch with my country. Even when I travel to India to visit my relatives, it no longer feels like home. It feels strange, and even the things I accepted earlier on in my life as okay now get me complaining and comparing. I am still thankful for my family staying together. Nothing can be better than that. It is the best price anyone can pay for, even for all the challenges of migration.

Nurse #4

My name is Maria. Am forty-five years old and from the Philippines, and my specialty is vascular and venous access. I have been a nurse for twenty-three years, five out of which I practiced in the Philippines. I migrated to the USA to join my family, and when I arrived, it was an easy transition because my sister and friends were already here and working in the hospital that hired me on an H-1B visa. I got much support from them with preparing for the boards, working as a CNA prior to taking the boards, and getting to know the community work environment and ethics. Even with all that support, I was challenged with cultural shock. It was so embarrassing and challenging to learn and accept the cultural differences of everyone at each level of interaction. Naturally, I am a quiet person, easily rattled by people with loud, boisterous attitudes. I am submissive and respectful to everyone. That was always taken advantage of by people, especially at work—my peers (as a CNA and even as an RN). I was not one who complained, so it was hard to speak up when I was overwhelmed with the patients given to me. I was, on some occasions, tearful and kept it all to myself except in the company of my family and my community. I am not feeling challenged anymore and am finally getting used to the environment and culture, being aware of everybody's behavior (patients and peers). I will consider my migration a success because I had the opportunity to get a job, earn some money, and stay with my family. My mother is here with us. Our dad passed away recently, but he refused to come for fear of flying in an aircraft.

Nurse #5

My name is Aditi. I am fifty-two years old from South India. I have been a nurse for twenty-four years, and my specialty is medical surgical nursing (twelve years in India). Regarding my migration, my husband was the motivator. He helped me apply for and successfully complete the CGFNS (the Educational Commission for Foreign Nursing Graduates test). He supported me all the way through the immigration process. The main reason for us to migrate here was for our children and a better future and opportunities. Some of the initial challenges were in my nursing practice. Although the patient care procedures were similar, I had to learn the procedures and familiarize myself with the policies. The biggest challenge was when my patients or peers used medical slangs, jargon, and abbreviations. I was unable to understand it, but I usually got assistance from my American colleagues and peers for interpretation. Also, the hospital had oriented nursing preceptors to train us (new immigrants) on the unit, which was very supportive. We were assigned Indian families as mentors to help us navigate through the cultural shock and environmental challenges. The hospital provided fully furnished apartments, including a week's groceries when we arrived. We were also supported by the church and members of our Indian community where we resided. The only challenge I had was as I was seeking admission to pursue my doctor of nursing practice (DNP) program. Since my nursing education had been completed in India, I was required to take an English course because only a few universities accepted our English credits from India and granted a waiver. I simply did not think it was fair, but I took the course because I was determined to pursue my career goal. I consider my migration a success. My family has grown. Our transition was very successful. I have completed and obtained my DNP and am presently working as a nurse manager with the hope of advancing my career to the next level. My husband and children are doing well, and we give God all the glory for this success.

Nurse #6

My name is Obiageli, Katherine. I am sixty years old from Nigeria. I have been a nurse for forty years, thirty-five years in Nigeria, and my background includes medical surgical nursing, operating room, and nursing administration. I was a CNO in my country and retired at the age of fifty-five years. It had always been my goal to migrate to the USA to make it possible for my children to get their education and career in this part of the world where different opportunities exist. It took me so many years to achieve it, but finally, it became a reality. When I passed my CGFNS examination, some of my colleagues back home who had migrated assisted in getting an agency to hire me through the H-1B visa. The agency came to Nigeria, and we all had to go for an interview, and through their agents in Nigeria, I got hired. That was when my first challenge commenced. I spent so much money paying the local agents to get information and paperwork for my immigration requirements, and most of the documents I had provided never got to the embassy, so I was never ever going to get an interview. After some time, the embassy called me to send my TOEFL scores and certificate. The local agents were not even aware of this correspondence. Meanwhile, they were asking for money to get me an interview date. I decided to go to the embassy and get more information for myself from this point on. I was able to take the TOEFL exam in an approved center, submitted my scores, and got an interview date.

When my visa was approved, some of my children had passed the age of twenty-one and were no longer approved to come with me on the H-1B visa. Eventually, I left Nigeria with just one of my children, and we arrived at our port of entry with no money. I was not sure who would meet us at the airport, even though my hiring agency had stated in the letter of contract to meet us at the airport and that they would give me accommodations and a job until I passed the licensing board. On our arrival at the airport, there was no one to meet us, and we sat at the airport lounge, hungry, confused, and not knowing what to do next. We waited for over eighteen hours from the time we had arrived, and no one came. We had no money to make calls. I was not sure how to call, but I had the phone number of one of my husband's relations living in another state, far from our point of entry. Fortunately, one of the workers at the airport offered to make the call for us, and within two hours, our relative was on his way to get us. It was very scaring and frustrating and such a huge disappointment. Finally, we arrived at his home and got comfortable but without a clue as to where to go or what to do next.

The initial challenge was how to meet up with or find the agency personnel who had hired me from my country. They made some efforts to reach the local agents in Nigeria, and through my husband, we made connection after a week. Then they arranged to get me and my child to relocate to another state but told me that the state would not allow me to work as a nursing assistant with my Nigeria RN license. Therefore, I was supposed to take the CNA test and pass it to get a job to support myself and my daughter. This offer was rejected, and my relative asked around, and we made connections with some of the people working in the hospital in the state we were presently residing in. We got a hospital to hire me based on the visa I had entered the country with, but there were some challenges regarding the change of sponsorship. It took almost four months to get the issue resolved, and it involved a lot of money. I was made to pay back the initial agency that had hired me before they released my papers to the new hospital. Then I started to work as a student nurse (nurse extern), and my child was enrolled in school. The next challenge was finding an apartment, which I was not eligible for because of my immigration status, credit checks, and background. The human resources department assisted me with the letter to clarify my immigration status, and some friends we had made from the church obtained the apartment in their name two months later.

I was also challenged with taking my licensing board exams after submitting my transcripts from my school back home to Worldwide

Education Services (WES) for evaluation. It took another eight weeks for them to conclude and send their recommendations to the Board of Nursing before I was given permission to take the tests. Of course, I failed the first test but passed it on the second attempt. It was not hard for me to transition to being an RN in the unit I was already working in. The technology, equipment, practices, procedures, patients, and families were not new for me.

The period when I had worked as a nurse extern made a huge impact because I followed the nurses closely when they performed their nursing tasks. As for my colleagues, the nurses accepted me and supported me in becoming a good nurse with the skills and knowledge required to do my job. The CNAs were every challenging. They either refused to take delegations from me or did such a bad job that they made me redo the tasks assigned to them for my patients. Sometimes I reasoned with them and decided to do the tasks myself instead of delegating them and returning to perform the tasks again. I was hesitant to report the issue to the charge nurse or nurse manager for fear of retribution, with them ganging up on me making my already stressed life worse. I suffered humiliation, discrimination, and bullying in silence, hoping to complete my one-year agreement with HR and leave the institution. I received wonderful support from the church community because from the onset, I had told my story and asked for support, which they wholeheartedly offered. Our church became my community, family, and friends. I am no longer facing so many challenges now because within a couple of years when I had gotten my citizenship, I filed the same for my family. By God's grace, they all arrived, and we are now staying together. I am not expecting to get back to becoming a manager or administrator because I am getting older and would rather spend money and time assisting my children to advance their education and career. My community has grown. I have been able to reach out to other friends from back home residing in the USA, and we have been visiting one another and having functions together. I will consider my migration a success because my initial aim to migrate is now fulfilled. My children are all here with me and pursing various areas of career advancement, getting married, and starting their own families. I know that my grandchildren will not have to go through thick and thin to become U.S. citizens. If there was a price for that, I paid it. On a personal note, it is a thing of joy to see how determination, hope, and faith can see one through the trials and tribulations of life. That is the success of my personal story, and I am grateful to God because He was with me and my child no matter what we had suffered. He had put people in place to assist us, starting from the cleaner at the airport of our entry. I have also been able to assist my parents, siblings, and friends back home as much as I can.

Nurse #7

My name is Ralph. I am thirty-eight years old from the Philippines. I was born and raised in Daquan City, a provincial city in the northern part of Central Luzon. I was a medical doctor in Manila, but the job and income were not enough to help me take care of my parents and siblings in the village. One of my friends told me that he was going back to college to take nursing courses and get a RN license. He said that would be the only way to migrate to the USA and improve our living conditions and assist our families more. I took the bait, sold some of my property, went back to college, and, within two years, got an RN license. We applied to take the U.S. licensing board exams (NCLEX) in Guam, and we were successful. Soon after, there was an interview by a hospital in Maryland that was sponsored by a top Philippine nurse in the USA, and so many of us went for the interview. Luckily, I was one of those who had passed and gotten selected and hired to depart to the USA. It was like a movie, but it was true and factual that within three years of my initial thought of migrating to the USA, it became a reality. My wife was a nurse, but she did not take the NCLEX but was granted her visa to travel along with me. All arrangements for our travel were made by the hospital that had hired us, and we arrived within a month and were welcomed by the hospital HR representative, the Philippine connection, and someone from the nursing department. They were so kind to us and had accommodations and food ready for us. We were introduced to other Filipino nurses working in the hospital, and that was very relaxing and encouraging. One of the greatest challenges I had faced was that we shared a two-bedroom apartment with another guy and his family, but we all had to make it work. I was also challenged on the nursing practice because I had never been a nurse and so was completely lost on how nursing stuff was done. My wife tried to coach me when I returned from work, but the hospital professional development staff were aware of our challenges, so they arranged for our orientation with fellow Filipino nurses on the unit assigned. From the onset, I told my preceptor that I did not have a nursing background, so he paid attention to my needs and gave me some slack if I made a mistake. He was a huge contributor to my success today as a nurse and did not push me or got angry when I did something incorrectly. The technology was not very new to me because as a medical doctor in my country of origin, I had an opportunity to use that equipment in the intensive care units, ERs, or critical care areas. I quickly learned to adjust to the things I did not know and had a lot of support from my preceptors and mentors. My nurse manager was very supportive and assisted me in adjusting quickly because she noted my ability to identify critical issues and results that could impact patient safety and to quickly point it out for intervention by the physician. I had a very good computer background (data collection and processing), and within one year, I was asked to join some committees like the one for nursing research. I am still challenged by one thing now, which is to try many times to separate my medical background from nursing. I have sometimes gotten into trouble by arguing with the physicians on what to do when a clinical situation comes up. I believe in myself and can fully advocate for my patients, but I have to operate within my scope of practice. I still want to go back and practice medicine, but the process of taking the medical board examinations, residency, etc. is not easy and may not be what I can do with my family growing and my folks at home to support. I will say that my migration is successful, but there are some regrets as well. The success story is that I have become integrated into the nursing practice here in the USA, working in the intensive care unit. My wife passed the boards and got a job, our family is growing, and the children are doing well in school. I was able to bring my mother, father, and mother-in-law here on a visit and spend some time with them. They were very happy and grateful, and I am still able to support them at home. I have been able to travel to and spend vacations in very nice places, which I do not think I would have been able to afford to do if I were still a doctor in Philippines. We enjoy a peaceful political climate here in the USA, unlike what is going on in my home country, although on some occasions, we are fearful for our family over there. My only regret is that I am not sure of ever following my childhood dream of practicing as a doctor again. For me, it is a part of my life that is still unfulfilled, and I deeply regret it every day.

A Second-Generation Immigrant Nurse

My name is Fatu. I am from Liberia. I am a second-generation immigrant nurse, and this is my story. My mother and stepfather, both nurses, migrated here to the USA through an asylum program because my country was fighting a civil war. My sister and I were left under the care of our aunt, which was a horrible period and experience for us. It was a period of two years, which felt like twenty years, before we joined our parents. My mom was a midwife whose license was not acceptable in the USA, so when she arrived, she had to go to school to get the LPN license, while my stepdad supported the family. After obtaining her LPN license, she started working in a nursing home and later got her associate degree in nursing and then her BSN.

I was eight years old when we had migrated, and it was not very difficult to transition to the school, community, and environment. I guess we were very happy to be reunited with our parents and go back to a normal school, life, and environment. After high school, my mom was asking me and my siblings to become nurses, but I wanted to be a pediatrician. I was not going to be a nurse after hearing all the stories of the challenges my mom and stepdad had been going through at work. Because I loved to take care of babies, the thought of being a pediatrician was my dream. I went online, searched for the steps of becoming a pediatrician, and discovered the years, finances, and requirements associated with it. It was very cumbersome and overwhelming. Then I changed gears and decided to become a pediatric nurse. My mom was happy. At least I would be a nurse first and specialize in pediatric nursing. I entered nursing school, and during my clinical rotations, I was face-to-face with pediatric nursing, and that caused me to have a change of heart. I could not do it. It was never what I had thought. Healthy babies are completely different from sick babies to hold. I have finished my MSN nursing program, graduated and holds a family nurse practitioner license. My two sisters eventually all ended up becoming nurses, so we are a family of nurses. I wish to say that my parents' migration is a huge success because they constitute today the support for our families back home. They offer financial, spiritual, and economic support for our families back in Liberia. My siblings and I have, in one way or another, assisted my mother in supporting our family back home and even taking care of her and our stepfather here in the USA. Also, her dreams of making all of us nurses worked out for her—a huge success. Does she have any regrets? Yes. She regrets that she missed a lot of opportunities to invest money and time in our home country, but all in all, she is happy with her migration and hard work as they all paid off in the end for her immediate and extended family.

Nurse #8

My name is Mabinty. I am originally from Sierra Leone but migrated to the USA from Northampton, England. My parents took us to England at a very young age. In fact, some of my siblings were born in England. We maintained a close relationship with our family in Sierra Leone, and as a result, even though I did not live there for a greater part of my life, I can attest and relate to their values, food, culture, and way of life. My mother was a surgical nurse, and from the time I had gotten to know that my mother was a nurse, she knew that my passion was for nursing, especially psychiatric nursing. At the age of five, the only thing I asked for my birthday present was a doctor tool set, and as soon as the present was given to me, I opened it and started listening to everyone's heartbeat and taking their temperature with my set. My mother could not understand my love for psychiatric nursing, but I know that at a young age, I developed a curiosity toward understanding the facts behind mental illness.

During some of the times we were back home in Sierra Leone, my curiosity increased because of the attitudes of the local people to mentally ill or challenged people. There was this myth and belief that mental illness was a curse from the "gods" or a reward or revenge for the evil that a family or person had committed. Most mentally ill people were either ostracized or left to die outside the family home. They lived in the marketplace or forest and did not have anything to do with the "normal people." Their families abandoned them, and no one cared for them. If they made attempts to return to their families, they were chased away and occasionally beaten up, and if they ever became agitated and violent, they were restrained using strong chains or ropes to tie them up. It has always beaten my imagination, why they have these health issues that have no cures and why society in my home country treats them that way. After high school, I went into nursing school, obtained an associate degree in nursing, and practiced in a hospital in Northampton. I worked in the psychiatric unit for a while and decided to migrate to the USA. Some of the reasons for my migration were career advancement and family issues that bordered on marriage and children. I came into the USA as a visitor, but got my status change through employment and my H-1B visa. It was slightly easier because I had come from the UK, settled in quickly, passed the nursing licensing board, and started to work as an RN. My children later joined me, and we have settled down with our lives and moved on. I have been working in the psychiatric unit, pursuing my life's ambition. There were some challenges during our transition, especially regarding cultural change. In England, where we were raised and lived, there was a slow pace of life. People were not so much in a hurry to get to where or do what they wanted. They were more patient, easygoing, soft-spoken, and friendly. When we came over to the USA, there was such a fast pace, with unfriendly people who were loud and occasionally little things triggering off anger and arguments. In school, the children faced some forms of bullying and discrimination. Another challenge was that the health-care system was different. The nursing practice used particularly high technology. In England, electronic health records (EHRs) were being used but not to the degree of what I encountered here. I am sure that presently, it must have improved or moved significantly if not equally, but I was able to navigate it easily because I already had some training in the modern use of EHRs. I will say that my migration is a success because if you set a goal and achieve it, then you can count your life as a success. Career advancement was my goal, and today I am happy to say that I really got my heart's desires. I obtained my BSN, MSN, and DNP (all in psychiatry), published a paper in psychiatric management, and was promoted to nurse manager for the inpatient acute psychiatric unit. My children have also done well in the various careers they have chosen and, probably from my influence, are pursing degrees and postgraduate degrees in psychiatric medicine. I have a stronger family now more than ever and have plans to travel to my home country in Africa one day to assist health-care providers and the community on problems of mental health. Above everything that has been part of my success story, I thank the almighty God for all He has done for me and my family. To Him be all the glory!

Many immigrant nurses like Ngozi have told their stories. It will be a good experience to hear the voices of some of the nurses who have come into contact with these groups of nurses and what their experiences were.

Nurses Who Worked with Immigrant Nurses and Their Experiences

Kim, Clinical Educator

Ten years ago, I oriented a new nurse from India. I will call her SK. She had been a star at her facility in India. Her clinical nursing skills were wonderful, but she had difficulty with the technology. At that time, we had Meditech as our computer documentation. She struggled as she attempted to learn how to navigate through the screens and review the patients' charts as well as document her assessments and medication administration. I worked with her one-on-one and put her through the documentation class three, maybe four times, but she was unable to assimilate the technology. SK was in her late forties or early thirties. She was placed on a performance improvement plan (PIP) and eventually fired because of the fact that she was unable to use the technology. She was very saddened by this and even showed me her badge that she had from her previous facility in India that showed that she was a "star" nurse. I think of SK often and wonder if there was anything more that I could have done for her. It saddened me that she was unsuccessful with the technology given as she had good clinical nursing skills.

Cheryl, RN

I had the opportunity to work with a lot of immigrant nurses hired to my unit in the acute care cardiac unit that I worked for over twenty-nine years. One thing I can tell you is that most of them came here with some good experiences, skills, and knowledge of what nursing is. They came from India, Africa, and Asia, and we could always see that the nursing practice is the same all over the world. I oriented most of them and watched them grow to become charge nurses, preceptors, and very skilled nurses whom we were proud to work with. The initial challenges we always encounter when they arrive are communication, cultural differences, and the use of technology. Initially, we find it hard to understand them, probably because of the accent (I am not saying it in a negative way), but you have to listen more closely to understand what they are saying. When we keep asking the same thing and they realize that we do not understand them, they feel bad and may quit communicating or do more writing. As we realize this, we do more writing reports and make them feel more acceptance than resentment. In fact, most of them give great care, but as you know, our patients (Americans) are more in tune to communicating with them as you give care, so they do not readily accept that the nurses do not freely communicate. They may ask for a change of nurse because they fear the nurse does not know what they are doing.

As time went on, we began to understand them, and they felt more confident to speak out and also picked up some American

English and accents. As for technology, computer, and practice, they put in their best and learned quickly, and that was a huge assistance. Culturally, they seem to be quiet and shy and cling to one another, like having lunch together and talking in their language sometimes, and that can be uncomfortable when you are working with them alone. As time progresses, the cultural difference becomes an asset to the entire unit as we get to do international potlucks, have fun together, etc. The country is getting close to having another nursing shortage, and immigrant nurses can be a huge assistance if possible.

Ruth, Director of Nursing

When we faced a nursing shortage in the mid-eighties and nineties, we resorted to hiring nurses from outside the country to meet our needs. It was a decision that was made out of desperation, especially since some of us had no knowledge about the training, skills, and knowledge of the foreign-educated nurses we would be recruiting. We were seriously concerned with the quality of care and patient experience. In 1980, Congress passed the Immigration Nursing Relief Act of 1989, creating the H-1B immigrant visa category for nurses, thus opening routes to grant visas to immigrant nurses. The lawyers went to town, most of them teaming up with some nurses from most foreign countries working here in the USA to operate agencies that would recruit these nurses.

The Commission on Graduates for Foreign Nursing Schools Inc. in Philadelphia played a major role because they were the first group to evaluate, test, and certify foreign-educated nurses whom we wanted to recruit. At least a U.S.-based organization that was founded by the American Nurses Association and the National League for Nursing has proven that the education, training, and skills of these foreign nurses make them able to practice in the USA. Based on this, my organization hired a lot of them, and it was pretty challenging. There became a need to get them oriented and acclimatized as well as help them communicate and understand our nursing processes and protocols. One of the challenges we had faced centered more on communication, cultural awareness, team collaboration, and technology. We hired quite a lot of them, and they were successfully transited to our practice. Today most of them have become our best nurses, educators, administrators, and practitioners. In my personal opinion, I do not mind doing it all over again if the need comes up, but most researchers have come up with research opinions that the utilization of foreign educated RNs lowered the practice of nursing, wages, and jobs for nurses born and educated in the US. I do not share their views, but I have no data or statistics to support my opinion.

CONCLUSION

It has been interesting, and fulfilling telling the stories of immigrant nurses, even up to their second generations, whose only tools and hopes in coming to the USA were their licenses, skills, and knowledge. For most of the migrant nurses, their nursing licenses and skills was not a big deal in their countries of origin, but they still persevered to leave, all for one purpose: seeking a better future. They came following the dream of making life better for their immediate and extended families, and they had huge success stories and a few failures. Most of them had given their successes or even failures to their faith and belief in the Almighty God, whom they have acknowledged led them all the way. Most of the stories that created "Aha!" moments were when it seemed that when there was a problem or things were going wrong, somehow something would happen, and a door would open for them to move on in their processes or needs. These migrant nurses believed that when they had left everything they had, knew, or would ever have to move to another country full of uncertainties, their lives were only directed at each level, as reflected in the hymn written by Fanny Crosby in 1875, "All the Way, My Savior Leads Me." The hymn, as found in the stories of these immigrant nurses, summarizes that the Lord provided them strength and guidance all the way through their journey.

Success means different things to different people. There is no one definition for success. It can mean the accomplishment of an aim or purpose or "knowing that what you are doing is helping you and others lead a better, happier, healthier life" (Kara Goldin, CEO of Hint Water). Success is not a "one size fits all" deal, and for me, success is knowing that my life is filled with the abundance of God's presence and grace. How can I describe my migration unless I stop and review the abundance of God in my life? As a Christian, I take the abundance of God in my life, reflecting the Word of God in John 10:10b—"I am come that they might have life and that they might have it more abundantly." My family enjoys the abundance of God's grace through various opportunities that the Almighty has placed in our lives. We have built sincere friendships in our neighborhood, church, community, and workplace. We made plans, and God blessed them and brought those plans to fulfillment according to His will. We have come to note the real purpose for the opportunity to migrate and that no matter what obstacles, challenges, or trials come our way, we overcome them. It was only by His grace and mercy, and for that, we shall ever remain grateful to the King of Kings.

Is nurse migration a thing of the past, or is there any hope for nurses from other countries ever migrating like their colleagues, whose voices you just heard?. One would think that with the advancement of technology and social media, it would be easier to hire nurses from abroad. On the contrary, it is more difficult now than before. Some of the barriers that presently impact nurse migration are the recession of the mid-2000s—which impacted almost all health-care organizations, reduced financial resources, and, much more, have halted or reduced the sponsorship and hiring of migrant nurses from outside the USA— and the long wait and backlog of green card applications related to the federal government lowering the cap on visas granted each year. In 2017, President Trump signed an executive order temporarily halting immigration, causing some confusion and concern in most countries. Although the temporary halt of migration was for seven countries alleged to have strong Jihadist connections, it also created some issues in other countries toward applications and job searches in America. Some Muslim nurses who had been applying for nurse migration had their applications immediately halted. Under the Trump administration, it has become more uncertain, what will become of foreign nurse recruitments, but most hiring agencies and hospitals have stated and encouraged nurses wishing to migrate not to be dissuaded by the new presidential executive order because there is still hope for foreign nurse recruitment in the future. Nurse migration is important to the USA, especially in the oncoming years, because of the expected huge exodus of experienced nurses and the looming retirement of the baby boomers. There will be another critical shortage of nurses. Therefore, the disruption of nurse migration to the USA would risk a health crisis. There exist some statistics that show impending nursing shortages. It has been noted that in some areas of the country, the demand of nurses will outpace the supply. For instance, the *U.S. News* published that "by 2025, Arizona, Colorado, and North Carolina are expected to be hit by the biggest nursing shortfall" (March 29, 2017). In 2017, there was a gathering of international health-care professionals in Dublin, Ireland, to discuss the worldwide health issues facing the globe. There was also huge concern about nurse shortage. They discussed a research paper that stated a projected shortfall of about eighteen million health-care workers worldwide by 2030, mostly nurses. The need to focus on reducing restrictions placed on nurse recruitment becomes imperative, especially when it was a successful tool used when global communities faced nursing shortages in the 1980s. Some of the research papers that have been published recently expressed this sad fact. In a publication in the *Hopkins Nursing Journal*, the writer, reviewing the global nursing shortage, expressed some concerns about the impact of nurse migration to the migrating countries. She stated that "this practice may be an obstacle to achieving the Millennium Developmental Goals, four of which directly relate to improving health care worldwide" (Walker, 2010, "Migration, Brain Drain, and Going Forward"). Taking this a little further and listening to the voices of the immigrant nurses in the previous chapter, it is important to see how nurse migration has impacted some of the countries represented by these migrant nurses whose voices we have heard. This is especially targeted toward improving health care in their countries.

Impact of Nurse Migration on Wushshi – my Home country

In addition to other factors that have impacted Wushshi as a country from making progress in achieving the UN Millennium Development Goals relating to health care, the country is also experiencing an extreme shortage of nurses to implement their programs. One of such programs is the Midwifery Service Scheme, which recruits midwives to work in rural communities and is hampered by the low availability of qualified midwives. The World Health Organization, in 2015, gave statistics showing Wushshi to have a ratio of 16.1 nurses and midwives per 10,000 in population against 88.0 in the UK and 92.9 in Canada (World Health Organization, 2015b). It is not an understatement to say that nurse migration has impacted, in no small way, negatively on health-care delivery in Wushshi. Many Wushshi scholars have published articles on this subject and highlighted how the migration of experienced and qualified nurses has slowed down and can slow down the pace and growth of Wushshi and African development. Based on several occasions when I visited and made contact with nurses at home and other African countries, the reality is that our next nursing generational workforce has a long way to go both in education and in professional practice. Most of the immigrant nurses have been touched in one way or another and have made several short term medical mission trips to Africa, with the sole aim of contributing to the healthcare of their people. Most of us are pushed by either guilt, spirituality, "giving back," or the economic returns of a 501(c) organization offering assistance, grants, etc. that come with their help. For whatever reasons, it is not enough. The knowledge, skills, and requirements to educate, train, and grow professional nurses are not reasonably accomplished within a week or month.

Some scholars have advocated the opposite of brain drain: brain circulation, which is described as the return of a migrant professional to their country of origin. They bring with them both human and financial capital acquired along the way to contribute and further economic development in their home country. This can be achieved through establishment of new businesses, partnerships with existing businesses, and building professional relationships. However, there exists some challenges that may face a migrant nurse returning to her home country, which include the acceptance of her new practice standards, the health-care environment, and the operating systems of health care in most African countries. It is really concerning if any of these initiatives can ever happen within my lifetime, considering the fact that some of the home governments show little or no interest or commitment to meet and improve the health-care needs of their countries. These governments need to commence and seriously address dilapidated health-care infrastructures and improve health-care operating systems and work environments. Until that happens, nurse migration or brain drain will continue, and this is sad for the countries we love dearly.